Henry Cecil was the pseudonym of Judge Henry Cecil Leon. He was born in Norwood Green Rectory, near London, England in 1902. He studied at Cambridge where he edited an undergraduate magazine and wrote a Footlights May Week production. Called to the bar in 1923, he served with the British Army during the Second World War. While in the Middle East with his battalion he used to entertain the troops with a serial story each evening. This formed the basis of his first book, *Full Circle*. He was appointed a County Court Judge in 1949 and held that position until 1967. The law and the circumstances which surround it were the source of his many novels, plays, and short stories. His books are works of great comic genius with unpredictable twists of plot which highlight the often absurd workings of the English legal system. He died in 1976.

HUNT
THE SLIPPER

by

Henry Cecil

HOUSE OF STRATUS

Copyright © 1977 Henry Cecil

This edition published in 2000 by House of Stratus, an imprint of Stratus Holdings plc, 24c Old Burlington Street, London, W1X 1RL, UK.

www.houseofstratus.com

Typeset, printed and bound by House of Stratus.

A catalogue record for this book is available from the British Library.

ISBN 1-84232-055-6

Contents

CHAPTER ONE

Reluctant Petitioner

It ought to be a source of satisfaction to many wives, even if they are of a jealous disposition, that their husbands show a healthy interest in other women. Those wives who say with apparent triumph: 'My husband never looks at another woman,' are unconsciously asking for commiseration. Although many of them may not realise it, the greatest triumph of a wife is to keep for herself alone a husband who has the normal polygamous instincts of a man. So the proper reply to a woman who boasts of her husband's fidelity in this way is: 'You poor girl. I'm so sorry.' For where is the triumph or the victory if there is no competition? Even in the first days of a marriage the new, adored little wife ought to be pleased to see her husband eyeing somewhat hungrily the face and figure of the woman at the next table. Provided, of course, that it is the wife who allays his hunger and not the woman at the next table.

In this respect Harriet Hunt had had no cause whatever for dissatisfaction with her husband, Graham. Almost from the first day of their marriage Graham showed a great interest in other attractive women, and although sometimes his interest may have been aesthetic or intellectual as well, it was basically sexual. But, up to the time he left her after twenty years of what had seemed to her an almost perfect marriage, she felt sure that, although he could have cheerfully slept with a dozen other women, he in fact reserved such courtesies for herself alone. Naturally when, without warning, he suddenly left her, she wondered at first with whom his affair could have been. It couldn't have been that beautiful girl whom they met in the South of France and whose body he eyed on the blazing beach with something of the look which he wore when he was about to drink his favourite soup. She was much too stupid, and more than once Harriet had heard Graham say that his urge to possess a beautiful girl would disappear like a pricked balloon as soon as she showed by what she said that her mind was empty of all the things which interested him. Oh yes, he could have functioned with her if they'd been alone together on a desert island or in some similar conditions but not otherwise.

Could it have been that dark-eyed girl with one of the most welcoming smiles which Harriet had ever seen, who could talk sensibly but not at too great a length on music, Jane Austen, the Bloomsburyites, tennis and rugby football, subjects in which Graham was very interested and quite knowledgeable? But they had only met her half a dozen times and, as far as Harriet knew, the last time was over a year before Graham left her.

On the 20th January 1976 Harriet had good reason for thinking about these things, for on that day she was to attend the Family Division of the Supreme Court of Justice for the purpose of obtaining a divorce from Graham, on the alternative grounds that he had deserted her or was dead. Although divorce has become all too common, it must be an emotional moment for many men and more women when the day comes on which the law is going to put an end to their marriage. Of course in some cases the emotion is almost entirely that of joy, joy at being released from a situation which had been for a long time quite intolerable, joy at finally being free from daily physical or mental assaults or joy at being allowed to live in virtue with a desirable new-found partner. But although Harriet intended to marry George Pennypacker when her decree had been made absolute, she was far from joyful as she considered what clothes to wear for her appearance in a court of the Family Division. For her love and affection and liking for Graham had never disappeared, even though his disappearance was now over seven years old. Harriet was a well-preserved fifty, vivacious, slim and attractive, with intellectual powers well above the average and with whom the desert island test should never have been necessary with any man. And it certainly had not been necessary with Graham, who had slept with her at first ecstatically and later most happily and successfully right up to the very night before he left her. Why had he suddenly left? Why had he said nothing about it? During the first month of his absence, when fruitless enquiries had been made through every possible agency, she began to believe that he must have been mugged and his body disposed of. But at the end of a month something happened which made her at first full of anger, for it seemed to show conclusively that he had left her quite deliberately and quite heartlessly. To leave a wife after twenty years of apparently happy marriage is bad enough but to do so without the slightest warning was unforgivable unless there was some extraordinary explanation.

It was exactly a month after his disappearance that Harriet received from a firm of solicitors in the Midlands a cheque for a hundred pounds with a letter which read as follows:

Dear Madam,

We are acting for a client whose name we are under the strictest instructions not to disclose. Upon his instructions we are sending you a cheque for a hundred pounds and should further inform you that at the end of each month hereafter we shall send you a similar amount. We fully realise there are many questions which you would like to ask us, but we can only tell you that there are no such questions which we shall be prepared to answer. We shall be obliged if you will acknowledge receipt of this letter and the enclosed cheque.

Yours faithfully,

PETTIFER & JONES

Harriet had no doubt that Graham must have been the solicitors' client, that he had gone off with another woman and was pensioning her off. She was furious.

Graham was ten years older than Harriet. He was an easygoing and amiable man whose manner concealed a high intelligence. He was extremely considerate and had always got on very well with Harriet. He had a dry sense of humour and a smiling face which would have been useful to any comedian. He had been in business as a paper manufacturer, and he and his three partners had resolutely refused to be taken over by any of the big companies. In consequence they had a good business but it was a small one. At the time when he disappeared in 1969 Graham's income varied between three and four thousand pounds a year. Although his ability was such that he could have earned a good deal more had he and his partners allowed themselves to be taken over, he appeared to find that his income was sufficient for his needs and to have little or no ambition to make a name for himself in the industrial world or to become a wealthy man. He sometimes described himself as a lazy man, and this was true to the extent that he would have been very happy not to have to earn his living but to be able to devote his entire time to his various outside interests and to his wife and home, but, when he had a job to do, he had to do it to the best of his ability. He and Harriet had never had a serious disagreement on any subject and, until he suddenly left her, she had felt quite certain that they both enjoyed their life together very much indeed. Indeed, while they were living together, she had never consciously thought about the matter, because it was quite unnecessary. Occasionally, however, like many happily married people, she indulged in a few self-satisfied thoughts. Such occasions were few and they were usually prompted by learning or reading about somebody else's divorce.

Almost from the moment when he left her (with an interval until her anger at the receipt of the hundred pounds had subsided) Harriet had kept up by herself her association with Graham. Even when she began to go out with George and when she realised what his intentions were, she did not give up her hope that one day Graham might return to her and that they would start again. Every night – except during what may be termed the angry few weeks – she prayed for his return. She did not pray to God but to Graham. Whatever he might have done, if he wanted to come back to her, she would forgive him without question. Well, perhaps not without question but certainly after the questions had been asked, whatever the answers were. Because, she said to herself, he wouldn't ask me to take him back unless he still loved me. So on this January morning, as she was considering what sort of dress the judge would like her to wear (because, like most petitioners, she wanted him to take a second look at her or at any rate to enjoy the first and only look) she had a futile hope that her petition might be dismissed. She felt sure that Graham must still be alive and there was always therefore a possibility of his return. But she could not go on for ever like this or without some solid hope, based on something concrete, that he would in fact return. George had now been asking her to marry him for nearly two years and at the end of that time she felt that it was not only unfair to George to keep him waiting longer but that it was unfair to herself not to start a more settled form of life. She was still sexually competent, George was quite attractive to her as a possible lover and she felt that she must not wait any longer. At first she had wondered whether Graham had left her when she was forty-three for fear that the time was coming when she would not be able to satisfy his sexual demands. But he was such a considerate man and such a considerate lover that, although at one time she had thought about this a lot, she could not believe that it was the truth of the matter. He must have gone off with another woman whom he preferred to her. But why had he not told her? They had always been at ease with each other and able to talk frankly on any subject. He would have known that she would have been hurt and probably angry, but it was not like him to leave her so that for a month she would not know whether he was dead or alive and after that time to pension her off like a discarded mistress with a sum which, although reasonable at the time when the solicitors started to send it, became wholly insufficient for her needs as the pace of inflation increased.

As she tried on one outfit after another, she thought how much she had enjoyed life with Graham from the very beginning of their marriage. They had been so happy together. They had laughed at the same jokes, revelled in Bach before breakfast and Mozart before dinner, enjoyed or hated or argued about the same plays, had the same taste in TV, enjoyed the country with its hills and birds and trees, were cheerfully critical of their friends and acquaintances and ate and drank and slept together with the near certainty that the future held for them plenty more eating, drinking and sleeping of the kind that they most enjoyed.

She eventually decided to go in a grey suit with a mauve scarf. It was not too smart for the occasion, but she had always looked well in it. And, having made that choice, she tried to concentrate on thinking of her life in the future with George.

She had breakfasted before dressing and was at the front door ready to go out to meet her solicitor and counsel outside the court, when she had second thoughts about the grey suit. She suddenly remembered that there was a green dress which Graham had loved and which she had never worn since he left her. It had now become fashionable again. She went upstairs again to the bedroom and eventually found it; she saw that it had been kept free from moth and she changed into it. She remembered how pleased they both were when she first wore it. They had lunched together in the West End to celebrate the nineteenth anniversary of their wedding day. She had worn it a lot during the ensuing year but not enough to make it shabby. And then it had been banished for seven years. So Graham, in the guise of the green outfit, would go with her to the Family Division.

CHAPTER TWO

Decree Nisi

Since the Divorce Reform Act of 1969 even the most fastidious judge can dispose of the majority of undefended divorces in a very few minutes. Before the law was altered some judges were prepared to turn a blind eye to something which the seeing eye of the law would not permit. The cases which most frequently required this kind of eye were cases of desertion. The law then required that, before a divorce could be obtained on this ground, one party had really to desert the other, but many members of the public thought that, if a husband and wife had been separated for three years, either of them was entitled to a divorce. It is not surprising that, if judges were prepared to assist in the bending of the law in these cases, some solicitors or barristers were also prepared to help in the process. But since the 1969 Act was passed an end has been put to these serious inroads upon the integrity of the law, for parties can *now* obtain a divorce by consent if they have been separated for two years.

So in the normal way Harriet's case would only have taken a few minutes. After all, there was no doubt that Graham had left her and he had been away from her for seven years. Even before the Act there would have been no difficulty in proving such a case, but in fact the judge set aside half a day for the trial of this case and there was a good reason for his doing so. The petition was based upon desertion or, alternatively, presumption of death. Graham had insured his life early in the marriage for fifteen thousand pounds and the policy was fully paid up. If Harriet had simply obtained a decree on the ground of Graham's death, this decree would not have been binding upon the insurance company. Even if in the Chancery Division she had obtained letters of administration or probate of his Will on the ground that he must be presumed to be dead, such proceedings would not have been binding on the insurance company unless they had been invited to take a part and had taken a full part in them. So, unless special steps had been taken, Harriet would have had to take at least two sets of proceedings, one in the Family Division for dissolution of marriage and the other in the Chancery Division for probate of his Will or letters of administration. If the insurance company had taken no part in those latter proceedings, she would have had to take further proceedings against the insurance company in order to establish her claim. In each of such cases she would have to prove one way or another that Graham must be presumed to be dead. It seemed to her lawyers that it would be ridiculous for legal costs to be incurred to this extent. Surely there could be a method by which, by one set of proceedings only, the insurance company could be fully heard and the question whether Graham was dead or alive could be fully investigated and a decision pronounced upon it. Accordingly, at the same time as they took the divorce proceedings they issued proceedings in the Chancery Division for probate of Graham's Will in which he had left everything to Harriet. At the same time they invited the insurance company to be a party to the proceedings and the insurance company readily agreed. They then applied to a judge in the Chancery Division to transfer the case to the Family Division so that it could be heard at the same time as the divorce proceedings. This was a most unusual course but the Rules of the Supreme Court did allow for it to be done. All the lawyers in the case, including the judge of the Chancery Division and the judge of the Family Division saw the good sense of this and it was arranged without difficulty. Although some people think that solicitors and barristers try to increase their incomes by making cases last as long as possible, for the most part both branches of the legal profession do all they can to keep the cost of the proceedings as low as possible and, indeed, to avoid the necessity for proceedings whenever this can be done satisfactorily.

This was why the case of *Hunt v Hunt* was the only case appearing in Judge Penberthy's list before lunch. The judge thought that it would be quite a pleasant change to have to consider whether the legal presumption of continuance of life would outweigh the presumption of death after seven years' disappearance and silence. Harriet was represented by Archibald Bugle, the insurance company by Stanley Meredith. Bugle was a man who practised in the Probate, Divorce and Admiralty Division before it was abolished by the Courts Act of 1971 and so he was not only familiar with divorce cases but with probate cases as well. This of course was an advantage to Harriet. But she suffered from the disadvantage that her counsel was a man who would seldom use one word if he could find two or two if he could find four. It was not often that you would find a divorce case which was going to take a whole morning and Bugle looked forward to the experience with some pleasure. Not because his verbosity would increase his fees but simply because he loved playing with words. And he would sometimes deliberately use an unusual word in the confident hope that the judge would have to ask what it meant.

'May it please your Honour,' he began, 'as you will no doubt have seen when you read the papers, this is an unusual case.'

'I have not read the papers,' said the judge.

'But your Honour is aware of how these proceedings come to be brought before you?'

'I know that the divorce petition has been consolidated with the probate action and that the insurance company has been given leave to take part in the probate proceedings. But of the facts themselves I know nothing.'

'I'm very much obliged to your Honour. I have to tell your Honour that the facts are in a small compass but that they are nevertheless somewhat unusual. I won't say that it is the most unusual case I have ever had but it is certainly one of the most unusual. And, if I may say so, I doubt whether my learned friend or your Honour has had such an unusual case to consider previously. I'm not of course saying that that's impossible. In my view it's very likely.'

'I'm not interested in your views,' said the judge. 'Nor does it help me in the least to be told, I think three times, that the case is an unusual one. I should be grateful if you would confine your opening to telling me what the facts are and drawing my attention to any law that may be involved.'

'I'm so sorry, your Honour, but I wanted to impress on your Honour's mind that it is not the sort of case which you would find it easy to deal with autoschediastically.'

Bugle paused for a moment and, as he had confidently hoped, he almost immediately obtained his reward.

'What was that word?' asked the judge.

'Autoschediastically.'

'What on earth does that mean?'

'In an offhand or extempore manner, your Honour.'

'Mr Bugle,' said the judge, 'do you use these unusual words to waste time or to show off your own knowledge?'

'It's an unusual case, your Honour, so I thought an unusual word might not be out of place.'

'I shall be grateful if in the future you will use more simple language while addressing me.'

Bugle for a moment wondered whether he would risk asking for a list of permitted words but quickly decided that that would be going too far.

'I will do my best to comply with your Honour's direction,' he said.

Bugle then told the judge, in as many words as he could find, the story of Graham and Harriet's marriage and how he suddenly came to leave without a word and without any further communication.

'But,' he went on, 'when I say "without any further communication" that is probably the real matter of difficulty which your Honour will have to consider. Your Honour has before you the letter which was sent to the petitioner with a cheque for a hundred pounds about a month after her husband had left her. A cheque for a similar amount with a covering letter has been sent to her every month since then, even up to last month. In spite of the fact that Messrs Pettifer & Jones said in their first letter that they would not be prepared to answer any questions, my client did herself telephone them to see if she could get any further information but was met with a polite but blank refusal. Subsequently her present solicitors communicated with Pettifer & Jones and a partner actually went down to interview Mr Pettifer. He was no more successful than Mrs Hunt. They have accordingly subpoenaed Mr Pettifer to give evidence before your Honour and, if I may say so with respect, it will be interesting to see whether your Honour is any more successful with Mr Pettifer than my clients were. As your Honour knows, the law is in my submission quite simple, namely this. That, if the petitioner proves that her husband has been away from her for seven years and that during that seven years she has had no reason to believe that he is alive, the Court will assume that he is dead. There would be no problem in this case but for the continuing remittances by the solicitors of one hundred pounds a month. Presumably this must have come from the husband, as my client will certainly tell you that she can think of no one else who could have sent it. The question your Honour is no doubt already considering is whether a lump sum of, say, ten thousand pounds was handed to the solicitors with instructions to send a hundred pounds a month or whether each month or, alternatively, every so often Mr Hunt gave Messrs Pettifer & Jones a hundred pounds to send on to his wife. I suspect that a satisfactory solution to this problem will only be achieved if Mr Pettifer is rather more forthcoming to your Honour than he has been in the past to my clients.'

Bugle went on for another ten minutes until the judge eventually said: 'Hadn't we better get on with the evidence, Mr Bugle? I know that I've allotted a half day to this case, but I don't want it to go over to the afternoon when I've a number of other cases to try.'

'If your Honour pleases,' said Mr Bugle, 'I will call Mrs Hunt.'

Harriet went into the witness box and was glad to see that the judge appeared to approve of her, or at any rate of her get-up, for, having looked at her while she was giving

13

evidence, he made a note in his notebook and then looked at her again.

Good, she thought to herself, Graham would have been pleased that I wore the green.

'Are you Harriet Louisa Hunt and are you the petitioner in this case?'

'Yes.'

'Where do you live, Mrs Hunt?'

'The Cottage, London Lane, near Redgrave, Surrey.'

'Is that your husband's house or yours?'

'It belongs to us jointly.'

'Were you married on the 9th day of June 1949 when your maiden name was Spicer to Graham Godfrey Hunt at the Parish Church, Redgrave?'

'I was.'

'I think that there are no children of the marriage?'

'That is so. We wanted children but unfortunately it was found impossible for us to have them.'

'Was it a happy marriage or otherwise?'

'Very happy.'

'I think that your husband was a paper manufacturer and had offices in London where he went every day.'

'That is so.'

'When did you last see your husband?'

'On the thirteenth of November 1968.'

'What happened then?'

'He went to the office as usual but he never returned.'

'Were you on good terms at the time?'

'Absolutely.'

'Had you had any quarrel of any kind?'

'None whatsoever.'

'Had he given you any warning that he was not coming home?'

'None whatever.'

'Were you aware of any other woman in whom he was interested?'

'I was not.'

'From the moment he went out on that day, have you ever seen him again?'

'No.'

'Have you ever heard of him again, either by telephone or letter or through a third party, other than from Messrs Pettifer & Jones?'

'No, I have not.'

'Was your husband's life insured?'

'Yes. He had a policy with the Birmingham Family Insurance Company Limited for fifteen thousand pounds.'

'Where was the policy kept?'

'With our bankers, the National Westminster, at their Redgrave branch.'

Bugle asked for the first letter from Pettifer & Jones to be handed to the witness.

'After you received that letter, did you communicate with Messrs Pettifer & Jones?'

'Yes, I did. I telephoned them and I asked – '

'No,' said Mr Bugle, 'you can't tell us what you asked. We merely want to know whether as a result of any questions you asked them you were able to get any information from them at all about your husband?'

'None whatever. They told me that they were under the strictest instructions not to answer any questions, as they had said in their letter.'

'Did you speak to the Bank about your husband?'

'Of course.'

'Were you able to get any information from them?'

'None whatever.'

After a few further questions Bugle sat down and Meredith got up to cross-examine.

'Do you believe your husband to be still alive?'

Bugle rose immediately, but before he could say anything Harriet said: 'Yes, I do.'

'Your Honour,' said Bugle, 'I object to the question and the answer. We have not yet reached the stage in the Courts when extrasensory perception is allowed to be taken into consideration. If there are any further facts upon which my client bases her belief, that is quite another matter. In my submission your Honour is not concerned with the state of my client's mind.'

'I quite follow that,' said the judge. 'No doubt that question was asked as a basis for further questions. Indeed, I will ask the witness the question myself. On what do you base that belief?'

'Partly the hundred pounds,' said Harriet. 'As far as I know, my husband had no other money except what was in his banking account and I do not see how he could have given in advance a sum of money which would have amounted to between eight and nine thousand pounds. So I assume that he was paying a hundred pounds each month.'

'You said "partly because of the hundred pounds",' said Meredith. 'What other reason?'

'Well,' said Harriet, 'there is another reason but I don't suppose you will take any notice of it in a court of law. I don't pretend that I'm a believer in ESP but my husband and I were very close to each other, very close indeed, and I have a feeling that he is still there somewhere.'

There was no further cross-examination and, after the bank manager had been called to say that he had had no communication with Graham since the day he left Harriet, that his account at that date was in credit to the amount of £203.25 and that, apart from the insurance policy, he had no other securities lodged at the bank and that he was aware of no other money possessed by Graham, Mr Pettifer of Pettifer & Jones was called.

After the formal questions about his position in his firm, a photograph of Graham was handed up to him and he was asked if he had ever seen him before.

'No.'

'Did someone give your firm instructions for a hundred pounds each month to be sent to Mrs Hunt and was the person a man or a woman?'

'Your Honour,' said Mr Pettifer, 'the person who gave my firm the instructions to send this hundred pounds made a condition of our being employed that we should in no circumstances tell anyone anything which might disclose the identity of the donor. Therefore, subject to your Honour's direction, I must decline to answer the question on the ground of privilege.'

'You can answer this question, can you not, Mr Pettifer, without breaking your client's confidence? Did you ever see the person yourself?'

'No, I did not.'

'Which member of your firm did see that person?'

'Mr Albert Jones.'

'Is he alive?'

'No, I'm afraid not.'

'Presumably you have a record at your office of the instructions given to your firm.'

'Yes, I have.'

'May his Honour see that record?'

'I have the record here,' said Mr Pettifer, 'but I have blanked out everything except the words "In no circumstances are you to disclose my identity or give any facts relating to this transaction to any person".'

The document was handed to the judge. 'How often,' asked the judge, 'did this person either come to your office or communicate with your firm after the first occasion?'

'Your Honour,' said Mr Pettifer, 'the answer to that question would involve breaking the condition of secrecy.'

'In what way?'

'Your Honour, if I said that the person only came to this office and only communicated with this office on one occasion, that would show almost conclusively that on that occasion we must have received a sum of money to enable us to pay a hundred pounds a month for a good many years. In other words, it would show that we received a lump sum. But, subject to your Honour's direction, I take the view that it would be a breach of confidence on my part to disclose whether these payments have been made as a result of our receiving a lump sum or whether we have received instalments from time to time.'

'Are you prepared to answer this question?' asked the judge. 'Have you any reason for believing that Mr Hunt is dead?'

The witness thought for a moment and then said: 'I think I can answer that question. The answer is No.'

'I shan't ask any further questions,' said Meredith.

Bugle at once got up and asked: 'Well, Mr Pettifer, have you any reason for believing that Mr Hunt is alive?'

'Subject to his Lordship's direction,' said Mr Pettifer, 'I'm not prepared to answer that question.'

'Why not?'

'Because in my opinion,' said Mr Pettifer, 'this would to some extent give some information about the transaction. If I have some reason for believing that Mr Hunt is alive it must be because he has communicated with my firm either by word of mouth or in writing and, if that were the case, it might suggest that he had paid us in instalments to enable us to pay the hundred pounds. And again, subject to your Honour's direction, I am not prepared to state whether he has or has not.'

'Well,' said Bugle, 'have you ever seen him or spoken to him or had a letter from him since you were first given the instructions?'

'Mr Bugle,' said the judge, 'you should not say "him". It might be "her".'

'I'm sorry, your Honour. Have you ever seen or heard from the person or had any communication with the person who gave you the instructions?'

'No,' said Mr Pettifer. 'But,' he added, 'you must remember that I didn't see him in the first place. So that personally until I was shown the photograph in court I did not know what Mr Hunt looked like.'

'Now,' said Mr Bugle, 'I ask this question subject to any objection from your Honour or my friend and I want to remind you, Mr Pettifer, before you answer it that we could, if necessary, subpoena everybody in your office to come and give evidence. Naturally we don't want to put you to that inconvenience. The question is: Has any member of your firm, as far as you know, had any communication either by telephone or letter or in person with the giver of your original instructions?'

'What do you say, Mr Meredith?' asked the judge.

'Well,' said Meredith, 'if I may retain my right to object to the question and answer in these proceedings, realising as I do the possible additional expense which may be incurred if the question is not answered at all, I will agree to its being asked and answered *de bene esse.*'

'That seems reasonable,' said the Judge. 'What is the answer, Mr Pettifer? Has anyone in your office to your knowledge had any communication with the person concerned who gave you the original instructions?'

'If I said No to that,' said Mr Pettifer, 'it would go a long way to showing that we were in the first instance given a lump sum, so I must respectfully decline to answer.'

'Well,' said the judge, 'where do we go from there, Mr Bugle? It seems to me that the witness is entitled to rely on his privilege.'

'We can't carry the matter any further,' said Bugle, 'so I would like to address your Honour.'

'Of course,' said the judge, 'but at the moment I must tell you that I am at present minded to grant a decree on the ground of desertion. I think that the regular payment of this money without any explanation is sufficient to displace the presumption of death which would otherwise follow from the lapse of seven years.'

'I hope your Honour will not be ephectic in this matter,' said Bugle, and paused in the hope that the judge would ask him what he meant by that word. He was to be disappointed.

'No,' said the judge, 'I won't be.'

'Forgive me,' said Mr Meredith, 'I'm afraid I don't share your Honour's and my learned friend's knowledge of the meaning of the word he used.'

The judge sighed. 'Why play into Mr Bugle's hands, Mr Meredith?' he said. 'As I didn't ask the question, he hoped you would, didn't you, Mr Bugle?'

'Of course,' said Bugle, 'and, to be quite frank, I must admit that I hoped your Honour wouldn't know the meaning.'

'For once you're wrong,' said the judge. 'I happen to know that ephectic means suspending judgment on a matter. But the fact that I know the meaning is no excuse, Mr Bugle, for your using it.'

'I'm sorry, your Honour,' said Bugle, 'but I thought it was rather a nice word to introduce into legal parlance. A nice short word to use for a judge who is inclined to reserve judgment.'

'Mr Bugle, if you waste much more time I shall ask the taxing master to consider whether counsel's fees should be reduced on that account.'

'Now,' said Mr Bugle, 'your Honour is being concionatory.'

'Have you anything further to add?' said the judge.

'Then your Honour knows – ' said Mr Bugle.

'Sit down, Mr Bugle,' said the judge, 'I'm not going to have any more of this nonsense.'

He then proceeded to give judgment in the case and to pronounce a decree of divorce on the grounds of Graham's desertion. He said that he was not satisfied with proof of death. When he had completed his judgment, Bugle got up and said: 'Might I ask your Honour a question?'

'What is it?'

'How will my client ever be able to get the money out of the insurance company?'

'I fully realise your difficulties,' said the judge, 'and, though I am not here to advise you about it, I think the answer probably is that, unless you go to the Court of Appeal and that Court takes a different view of the evidence, your client will have to wait quite a long time, unless she can obtain further evidence to show that a lump sum was paid to Messrs Pettifer & Jones in the first instance. Mr Hunt, if alive, is now sixty years old. There being no evidence that he was not in a perfectly good physical state of health, I should say that in a little over ten years an application to presume his death might be more successful, for he will then be over the three score years and ten suggested in the Bible as the normal term.'

'But was he a man of great strength?' asked Meredith.

'That will do for the moment,' said the judge. 'I shall rise now.'

A few minutes later Harriet thanked her solicitors and counsel and was on her way to meet George Pennypacker to celebrate the granting of her decree nisi. But she didn't feel much like celebrating and was glad that she would still be wearing Graham when she met George.

CHAPTER THREE

Bed for Two

George was waiting for her at the restaurant and his eyes lighted up when he saw her. He did not give quite such a good performance as Mary Astor in Dodsworth, but it was quite effective and was not lost on Harriet. It made her feel sorry for him, for she knew that, although she was prepared to marry him and to be a good wife in every way, her heart would still be with Graham, whether he was in heaven or in hell or even if he were living in Southsea with a bright little blonde. But she responded to his obvious happiness by kissing him fairly and squarely on the mouth and letting her lips linger there for a few seconds.

'All went well?' asked George.

'Yes,' said Harriet, 'except that we shan't get the insurance money yet.'

'I wonder how long the hundred pounds a month will go on,' said George. 'Did Pettifer give any indication?'

'None at all.'

'Oh well, it can't be helped. Let's go and have a drink.' They went to the bar of the restaurant and were soon toasting each other with two dry Martinis. 'Darling,' said George, lifting his glass.

'Darling,' said Harriet, doing the same, and then after the first sip she said: 'What does concionatory mean?'

'Come again,' said George. Harriet repeated the word.

'I haven't the faintest idea. Why d'you want to know?'

'My counsel used the word and it seemed to make the judge angry. What d'you think it means?'

'How's it spelt?'

'I've no idea.'

'If it's spelt c-o-n-s-c I suppose it's got something to do with conscience. But how did he come to use it?'

'He was just trying to annoy the judge,' said Harriet. 'It's of no importance. D'you think we ought to give a party?'

'That's just what I was going to talk about. Yes, I'm all for a party. Not too many though. Thirty or forty, d'you think?'

'Not more,' said Harriet. 'It depends where we give it. We'd better have it at the cottage. It's much too expensive to go to an hotel.'

'I don't know how they manage these days,' said George. 'Yet most places always seem to be full. But, if it's a fine day, it would be lovely in the garden and, if it's wet, we could get thirty or forty people in the two rooms combined. Most of them will be standing all the time.'

'When shall we give it?' asked Harriet. 'Before my decree is made absolute or after?'

'Whichever you like, darling,' said George. 'Perhaps afterwards would look better. It would be pretty awful if Graham turned up before we were married.'

'D'you think he might?'

'Of course not. He's as dead as a doornail.'

'The judge didn't seem to think so. And anyway why should he be? He has always been in good health. He's only sixty.'

'Well,' said George, 'there's one good thing. He's dead to you, at any rate, or you wouldn't be marrying me.'

24

Harriet said nothing but made a sort of stroking movement with her right hand on her dress. George noticed the fact but didn't say anything.

'That's right, isn't it?' he said.

'I'm sure we shall be very happy,' said Harriet.

'I'll do all I can,' said George. 'After all, we've known each other pretty well for the past two years and we don't seem to irritate each other too much.'

'I've never asked you this before,' said Harriet, 'but why didn't you get on with your first wife?'

'I don't really know,' said George. 'She was a nice girl and we had many of the same tastes but I fell out of love with her, I suppose.'

'What d'you mean by that?'

'If you want to know, after six months I found it difficult to go to bed with her and after a year I just couldn't manage it. So it didn't make it any easier that we had a double bed. And I was always grabbing the sheet when she wanted it.'

'Well, we can agree on that,' said Harriet. 'I like my own bed.'

'Good,' said George, 'but I hope I'll be welcomed there sometimes.'

For the first time Harriet gave George a loving smile. After all, she said to herself, in my heart of hearts I know that Graham will never come back. I'm very fond of the sexual side of married life and I've been starved of it for seven years. I might as well enjoy myself while I get the chance. What does it matter if from time to time I think of Graham looking at us with an encouraging smile? Graham was like that. He wouldn't be angry. He'd be pleased for her to be happy. She was fifty. She could hear Graham saying, 'Enjoy yourself while you're young, my dear.' But, she reflected, she would not take the same view of

Graham lying next to his blonde in Southsea. She finished her drink.

'Can I have another, please?'

'Two more dry Martinis,' said George. Harriet gave him another of those smiles which made him wish that the decree absolute had already been granted. He said so.

'Are you longing for the party all that much?' asked Harriet.

'You know what I'm longing for,' he said.

'Darling, so am I.'

'D'you mean it?'

'Of course I do.'

'D'you think we need wait?' As Harriet didn't answer, he said: 'Give me one solid reason why we should. It's not like it was fifty years ago and even if people learned about it – and there's no reason why they should – practically no one would think any worse of us. I've been waiting for it so long, darling.'

'All right,' she said suddenly. 'Tonight.'

'D'you mean it?'

'Of course I mean it. Come to the cottage at seven o'clock and we'll have a couple of drinks and go to bed. And at half past nine I'll have a nice little supper ready.'

'It sounds wonderful.'

'But, if we're going to do all that, we'd better go into lunch, otherwise there won't be time for me to get back to Redgrave and do a certain amount of shopping and cooking. Then I shall want a rest.'

They got up and went into the restaurant and sat down at a table.

'D'you know,' said George, 'I don't feel hungry any more. I keep thinking about seven o'clock tonight.'

'Seven thirty,' said Harriet. 'Don't forget the couple of drinks. Well, I'm starving,' she added. 'Do get the waiter.'

When they had ordered the food, Harriet returned to the subject of George's first wife. 'You never told me what actually happened,' she said.

'Well, she wasn't too pleased when I suggested having separate rooms and from that moment we started to bicker and after a couple of years of this we decided to pack it up. I suppose, when you come down to it, it means that we were sexually incompatible.'

'How d'you know we shan't be?' said Harriet.

'I'm sure we won't but that's all the more reason for trying it out, isn't it?'

'You didn't discover it for six months.'

'I'm sure we shall be all right, darling,' said George.

'But nothing in the world is certain. Even people who are fantastically in love may find that they don't suit each other sexually. I don't want to find that after six months you don't want me any more,' said Harriet. 'I'll be nearly fifty-one then. I don't want another divorce. We don't want to be technical about it or bring out slide rules or anything of that sort but the more I think of it the more I like the idea of having a try-out first so that we may at least have some idea whether we like it or don't.'

'Don't say that,' he said.

'But you and your wife liked it at first, didn't you?'

'Yes, I suppose so. Can I ask you something?' said George.

'What is it?'

'Darling, would you like me to be gentle or rough?'

'You'll be doing it by numbers next,' said Harriet. 'I just want you to be yourself.'

'But I like to be considerate,' said George. 'There can't be any harm in that. I mean, if I treat you as though you could easily break up like a well-made meringue and all

27

the time you want me to behave like a ferocious polar bear, you wouldn't be best pleased.'

'I can say at once,' said Harriet, 'that I don't want you to knock me about.'

'I wouldn't dream of doing that,' said George.

'Why do you mention the ferocious polar bear? I don't want you to break my ribs either. By the way, did you talk like this to your first wife before you were married?'

'No,' said George.

'Why not?'

'It never occurred to us.'

'When you found you weren't getting on, did you go to the marriage guidance council?'

'No. I did think of it but there didn't seem any point really. We did try for a couple of years. So there wasn't really any advice they could have given us.'

'I hope it will be all right,' said Harriet. 'I won't say this again because it might hurt you. You see, I've got a very happy marriage to look back on. Everything went right from the start.'

'You mean,' said George, 'that things could only be worse between you and me.'

'That's a horrid way of putting it,' said Harriet. 'I suppose it's true. Whereas from your point of view they could only be better.'

'And what all that comes to,' said George, 'is that the whole time I'll be in danger of your saying what a much better husband Graham was.'

'You've got to face up to that,' said Harriet. 'No one in the world is perfect and, although Graham had lots of faults, from my point of view he was as near a perfect husband as a man can be. He lived life so easily. He was the most adorably casual man that I've ever known.

Nothing ever seemed to worry him. He was such a happy man and he made me such a happy woman.'

'He *was* a facetious devil,' said George.

'I suppose he was,' said Harriet, 'but his kind of facetiousness was never annoying. He never used it at the wrong time, for instance if I dropped an iron on my toe. When I come to think of it, when I dropped it on his toe once, he made a joke of it which is more than I should have done.'

'I don't suppose you'll drop one on mine,' said George. 'Lightning never strikes in the same place.'

'It does, you know,' said Harriet. 'There was a case in the paper the other day. A chap sheltered under a tree which had been struck by lightning and he was badly burnt when it got struck again.'

They ate for a few minutes in silence and then George said suddenly: 'You wouldn't like to call the whole thing off, I suppose? You seem so obsessed with the happiness of your first marriage and the virtues of Graham that I don't seem to stand much of a chance if you're going to be thinking of him all the time and then comparing me with your ideal husband.'

'That's perfectly fair,' said Harriet. 'There is a danger. But I'm prepared to risk it if you are.'

'Then you must want me to some extent.'

'Of course I do.'

'Is it simply because you want a man?'

'That's a cruel way of putting it.'

'But I would like to be sure that it's *me* you want.'

'Of course it's you. But with a second marriage there's always a danger. If the first has been quite superb, the second may fail by comparison. And you will be taking the risk more than me. Are you still prepared to take it?'

29

'You mean,' said George, 'that you're prepared to have me as a second best, if I don't mind being treated as a second-rate substitute.'

'Not second-rate,' said Harriet. 'That isn't fair. But I must admit that no one could be to me what Graham was. I don't mean that he was such a good man, but he made such sense of everything. I don't think anyone could have been unhappy with him.'

'But they might with me?'

'Of course they might, as you might be with me. You see, I think that Graham could adapt himself to anyone. But I certainly couldn't.'

'I've always thought that I was pretty adaptable,' said George.

'I think you are but I'm not.'

'I'm quite prepared to spoil you,' said George.

'That's nice up to a point,' said Harriet, 'but Graham did it without it appearing an effort.'

'Why should I find it an effort if he didn't?'

'You'll soon find that out. I'm a very ordinary woman. I've got quite a good temper but I'm extremely jealous and I'm as illogical as most women.'

'But you don't sulk?'

'No. I don't think so. When my tantrum's over I'm prepared to forget it. I suppose that was Graham's only failing. He did occasionally sulk if I got in a temper. It was his method of defence. And I could always tell when he was sulking. Not because of anything that he said, because on those occasions – and there weren't many – he'd bring out a pipe, carefully fill it and press it down, bring out a box of matches, take out a match and, without striking it, put it back again in the box. And then he would replace the pipe in his pocket and, when he'd done all that, he'd speak to me again as though nothing had happened. I suppose it was his method of counting ten.'

'The whole thing could only have taken three or four minutes,' said George. 'Not more than five or ten anyway. Not much of a sulk.'

'I didn't say it was.'

'Well,' said George, 'I haven't got a quick temper and I don't think I sulk either, so I've got one over Graham there.'

'I expect you've got a lot of virtues that Graham hadn't.'

'I'm glad you said hadn't.'

'I meant to say hasn't. I tell you that he wasn't a paragon. I expect he had wicked thoughts the same as we all do from time to time. And I expect that he did as many bad things as the average person does in this life. It's simply that I can't bear the thought of being married to anyone else. Now, what have I said?'

'If you mean it,' said George, 'we'd better cry the whole thing off.'

'I don't know what made me say it. If that's how I really feel, it doesn't look as though it would be fair to you to go on with it.'

'You know, this really is a bit thick. You've led me on for months. Oh yes, I know that you were still hankering after Graham, but when you decided to divorce him, I really thought you meant to cut your losses.'

'I'm sorry, George. You're perfectly justified in being angry. It was a stupid thing to say. I must have hurt you.'

'I'm not angry. I just don't understand. We arranged this lunch to celebrate your decree, and we spend most of the time saying what a wonderful man Graham is, or I prefer to think, was. Of course he was a wonderful man – worth ten of me any day – but I might remind you that after twenty years of marriage he dropped you like a hot potato.'

George stopped talking to Harriet and called the waiter. 'Can I have my bill, please.'

'I hate ending this way,' said Harriet. 'Don't let's. I really never intended to say what I did. Dear George, I'm very fond of you and I'd love to go to bed with you. Even if you're angry.'

'D'you mean that?'

'There's no doubt about that at all. And if it's any consolation to you, I've often imagined myself in bed with you and wondered what it would be like.'

'Then you don't want to cancel tonight?'

'Not unless you do.'

'I tell you what,' said George. 'What d'you think of this? Cut out the idea of marriage for the moment but keep the appointment for seven o'clock. You may think that sounds a bit sleazy but it might be better in the long run. If we go on happily like that for six months or so, we can reconsider the matter.'

'Would that be fair to you?' asked Harriet.

'Perfectly. Putting it crudely, it means that I shall be getting a mistress instead of a wife. And a very beautiful one at that. And it won't be my choice that you're not a wife.'

'What could be fairer than that?' asked Harriet. 'What d'you think you'd like for supper tonight?'

CHAPTER FOUR

Parson's View

Having disposed of this little matter George and Harriet finished their lunch in a much better frame of mind. But on the way home Harriet was again filled with doubt, and she badly wanted to consult someone. The person she really wanted to consult was Graham. He would have given sensible and considerate advice and probably would have been right. To whom could she go? She was not a regular churchgoer and, although she'd met her local parson, she did not know him at all well. She wished she could have consulted a man like Sydney Smith. She felt sure that he would have given her robust and sensible advice, for, although he lived at a time when adultery and fornication were words that could hardly be used in polite society, his writing showed that he was a broadminded man. Much of what he had written and preached could have been written or preached at the present day. But there was not much time to get advice because she had to shop and do some cooking before seven o'clock.

Suddenly she made a decision. She would forgo the little rest she had promised herself. She had read in the paper a letter which she thought was very sensible. It was from a parson and was about a decision of the High Court which dealt with the position of a mistress from the legal point of view. The writer's living was in London, she looked his name up in the telephone book and immediately telephoned him. Fortunately he was in and he agreed to see her at once. His name was the Reverend Stanley Kewthorpe and fortunately he lived near Victoria.

'It's extraordinarily good of you to see me,' she said when he answered the door himself.

'If I can be of any help, I'm only too pleased.'

'I'm not a regular churchgoer but I am a member of the Church of England and I have a problem.'

She told him what it was.

'Please don't think I intend to be unfriendly or unkind,' said Mr Kewthorpe, 'but what you're really seeking to do is to transfer the responsibility from yourself to me. Only you can make a decision in this matter.'

'But surely you can give me some guidance. Of course I must take full responsibility for whatever I do and, when I answer to God on the great day of judgment, if he is displeased with what I have done I shan't say, "Oh but Mr Kewthorpe told me to do it".'

'Are you a Scotswoman by any chance?'

'No, but I once heard someone in court take the Scottish oath and I have always remembered the words "As I shall answer to God on the great day of judgment".'

'Yes,' said Mr Kewthorpe, 'they're even worse in Scotland than they are here.'

'But,' said Harriet, 'if the witness really thinks what is meant by that phrase, surely it may impress the necessity to tell the truth on his mind even more than the English oath.'

'Certainly if the rest of the oath were couched in sensible terms or in terms with which the witness could comply. When you obtained your divorce you swore that you would tell the truth, the whole truth and nothing but the truth, not that you would do your best to do this but that you would actually do it. In many cases witnesses don't know what the truth is. In some cases they are obviously mistaken as to what the truth is and in all cases they must know that they may make an actual mistake in what they say. Forgive my burdening you with one of my hobby horses but I was a barrister before I became a parson, and I also know that the laws of evidence often prevent a person from telling the *whole* truth. Yet he has sworn by his God that he will tell it. Which is the more important, Almighty God or the little man who is decked up in the uniform which the law provides so that you shan't see what he really looks like? But I mustn't go on. I'm sorry. The first question is, should you marry a man whom you feel you can't marry as long as there's the slightest possibility that your husband is alive and might return to you. That's right, isn't it?'

'Yes.'

'Well, there's no difficulty in answering that question, is there? The answer is obviously No. And I'm not saying that because the Church might consider that the intercourse ensuing upon the second marriage might be adulterous. I'm saying it, because it wouldn't make sense. I think your own belief that your husband ran off with another woman is in the highest degree likely to be correct. I also think that the probability is that he is still alive. He certainly behaved in an extraordinary fashion for a man of the character which you attribute to him. But the strangest things do happen in human affairs. You told me that your husband described himself as a lazy man and has often said that he would prefer to do nothing at all except enjoy himself. This may well have been the case. It is quite possible that he has run off with some woman of considerable means which has enabled him to do this very thing. That would account for his immediate payment to you of a hundred pounds a month.'

'But if he's still alive,' said Harriet, 'why hasn't he increased it? If he's got plenty of money he must know that a hundred pounds a month is nothing like enough to enable me to live.'

'Now or for some time past he might well have increased it,' said Mr Kewthorpe, 'but his failure to do so is not all that surprising. For, after all, by leaving you without a word he behaved in a disgraceful manner which you say is quite uncharacteristic. His failure to increase the monthly allowance is far less blameworthy than that. And, if he's a lazy man by nature, he simply may not have bothered. He might have put you completely out of his mind by paying enough money to the solicitors to send you the hundred pounds for many years and he has considered that part of his life closed. So that is I think the probability, that he is alive and well and living happily with another woman. And it is quite likely that she is a woman of means. At any rate, whether I am right or I am wrong in my belief, you can't deny that it's a fair possibility that this is the case. In those circumstances it is always physically possible that he will return to you. You would obviously like this to happen and, therefore, personally I think it would be quite wrong of you to get married again, even though the person to whom you were married is fully aware of all the circumstances. I do not believe that either you or he would have lasting happiness in such a marriage. And furthermore, although it is unlikely that your first husband will come back, it is not impossible. What would happen if he did? Would you still feel the same about him if he really wanted to come back to you? You would all three be in a mess. I've no hesitation in giving you advice on the first matter. But in doing so I realise that I am preaching to the converted. It's a decision that you've already come to yourself. You felt you wanted it confirmed by someone who knew neither of you, and I have no hesitation in saying that I think you are absolutely right.'

'Thank you, Mr Kewthorpe,' said Harriet. 'I am grateful to you and I am glad you've said what you have. And now about the second matter. What's your view on that? Can I decently become his mistress?'

'What on earth do you mean by "decently"?'

'Sorry,' said Harriet. 'I withdraw the word. Can I become his mistress?'

'Of course you can.'

'I mean should I become his mistress? Would I be doing a great wrong if I do?'

'Wrong to whom?'

'To myself or to God – or to Graham?'

'What do you mean by God? Everyone has a different idea of God. But if you mean the God of the Bible and the Prayer Book and the God whom every church has to some extent to personify for the benefit of the people who come to church, then it's pretty plain that fornication is not approved of by that God.'

'But Christ said: "Let him who is without sin among you – ".'

'That has nothing to do with it,' said Mr Kewthorpe. 'Christ was dealing with the question whether one man was qualified to punish another and he pointed out that he was not. But that the woman had sinned was taken for granted. And you will remember that Christ added, "Go and sin no more".'

'But that was a case of adultery, not just fornication. There's nothing in the Ten Commandments about committing fornication.'

37

'You ought to have been a lawyer,' said Mr Kewthorpe. 'But there's plenty of authority in the New Testament against fornicating.'

'Surely,' said Harriet, 'that was only by Saint Paul. And he was a man. There's nothing in the Gospel against it, is there, nothing by Christ himself? And you will remember that Saint Paul said a number of things about women which are not accepted today, even by those who disapprove of women's lib.'

'You're quite wrong about fornication only being disapproved of by Saint Paul. Christ himself said, "Out of the heart proceed evil thoughts, murder, adulteries, fornications, false witness and blasphemies. These are the things which defile a man." '

'So on behalf of the Church of England you disapprove of my sleeping with George, unless I marry him.'

'The Church of England would disapprove of your marrying him or sleeping with him,' said Mr Kewthorpe. 'But that is not necessarily the advice that I shall give you.'

'Oh?' said Harriet in a surprised tone.

'I don't think one must be too technical about these matters,' said Mr Kewthorpe. 'I suppose that a Roman Catholic priest would have to tell you not to do it again if you went to confession and told him about it. I really don't see what else he could do. But I personally think there are other things to be considered. It seems to me that, if you go on seeing George and don't sleep with him, both of you are likely to become frustrated. A frustrated person is far less likely to be a good neighbour and a happy one. It would be a great strain on you both if you go on seeing each other without getting into bed from time to time. Indeed, you will probably indulge in what is sometimes called "heavy petting". From a moral point of view that is just as bad as full fornication. Indeed, in a way it's worse, because the failure to complete the full sexual act would be a form of hypocrisy. Now, you've only just come to me and put this problem, so I am thinking aloud to some extent. It seems to me that for the sake of your souls and for the sake of the people whom you each meet in your daily lives, you should either give up seeing each other altogether or you should yield and yield freely and without a sense of shame to your natural inclinations. From the purely human point of view I think that much more than good will be done if you go on seeing one another and never make love. So I think the question resolves itself into this. Should you go on seeing each other or make a clean break? What's your answer to that?'

'I think,' said Harriet, 'that's the advice I wanted you to give me. Although it won't be easy to take, unless I act purely selfishly.'

'You mean, I suppose, that if you go on seeing George and sleeping with him, he won't have the opportunity of falling in love with some other woman who is in a position to marry him.'

'Exactly. And it isn't the same for me. For, as long as I feel that I'm still married to Graham, I wouldn't want to marry anybody else who came along, any more than I now want to marry George. So I shouldn't stand to lose and George will.'

'I think,' said Mr Kewthorpe, 'that George is old enough to make the decision for himself.'

'But he may hope that I shall actually marry him.'

'And indeed you may. No, I think you can treat yourself and George on equal terms.'

Neither of them said anything for a few minutes and then, after a little thought, Harriet said: 'If we were your parishioners and you knew all about us, would you give us Communion?'

'Well,' said Mr Kewthorpe, 'you'd certainly be in love and charity with your neighbours, but, on the other hand, if your sleeping together constitutes a sin and you did not repent of it nor indeed intend to lead a new life, I would still have no hesitation in giving you Communion myself. But I expect that there are some other parsons who would feel that they had to stick more closely to the rules. They would willingly give you Communion if you were about to break off your association but, if you made it plain that you were going to continue it, I think that some of them would at least be reluctant and some would definitely refuse.'

'Then, on the whole,' said Harriet, 'you won't think badly of me if I carry on with our proposed programme for tonight?'

'In the ordinary way,' said Mr Kewthorpe, 'I only think badly of people who deliberately do harm to other people. As far as I can see, the only people you would be doing harm to, if you would be doing harm at all, would be yourselves. I think it is a very healthy sign that you are giving so much thought to the matter, and although in the end you felt that you wanted an outsider to make it easier for you to do what you really wanted to do, I am very glad to be that outsider. I suppose, if fornication were a criminal offence it could be said that I was a party to the crime. Counselling and procuring, I think they used to call it. Well, I may not be procuring but I am certainly counselling. And the best of luck to you both.'

Harriet left Mr Kewthorpe very happily.

'I expect this is how a Catholic feels after a really good confession,' she said to herself. Then she tried to think what they would have for supper. But at first she found it difficult to concentrate. Going to bed with George was going to be a great moment in her life. She had been starved of sex for seven years. And now she was going to enjoy it again. She knew that Graham wouldn't mind. But, my God, what a nerve if he did. He's been enjoying it with someone else for years. Even in imagination she was not going to have him minding. 'That's all right, darling,' she made him say, 'enjoy yourself. You deserve it.' Well, she did deserve it. She'd waited for seven whole years and she was now fifty. Yes, she was certainly going to enjoy it. She started to visualise herself with George in bed and part of her pleasure was in a way getting even with Graham. But it must be a success. She felt sure it would be. It had got to be. At that stage she decided she must snap out of it. 'I think we'll start with smoked salmon,' she said to herself. She was a good cook and able to produce comparatively cheaply a meal which would cost a great deal in a restaurant. When she had finished her shopping, she felt happier than she had for a long time.

She managed to get an earlier train than she had expected for Redgrave. She picked up her car at the station car park and was delighted to think that George had agreed to her suggestion that they would go to bed after drinks and have supper later. The time which they would take over a couple of drinks would be just enough to increase their happy expectations. But a carefully prepared supper before going to bed would be completely wasted. They would want to get through it as quickly as possible and would take very little notice of what was in it. On the other hand, when they had satisfied themselves in bed it would be a very pleasant satisfaction of a different kind to be able to enjoy at leisure the meal which she would prepare. She was singing happily by the time she reached the cottage.

The cottage in fact consisted of two cottages which had been converted into one. It had two sitting rooms, one of which was immediately behind the front door. They called it the hall and the one which led out of the hall they called the sitting room. She put the car away and let herself into the hall still singing. She noticed nothing particular as she walked in and shut the front door, but, as she was shutting it, a voice suddenly spoke. It was Graham's. He was sitting in an armchair, with a book on his knee, and, as Harriet came in, he looked up from the book and said: 'Hullo, dear. I'm back a bit early. There's a strike on, so there wasn't much point in my staying in the office.'

Harriet nearly jumped off the floor.

CHAPTER FIVE

The Return

Graham was sitting comfortably in the armchair with the book on his knee, just as though he'd not been away from home at all. In the few seconds of silence which followed the shock which Harriet had sustained she was able to see that he looked very much as he did when he left her, except that he looked a little older and rather thinner, but there was still the happy, incipient smile on his lips. Her first instinct was to rush to him and hug him and never let him go. But before she could act upon this instinct a sudden wave of anger hit her. Graham had obviously left her for another woman, spent seven whole years with her and then, if you please, when she was dead or no longer sufficiently attractive to him, had come home with an air of arrogant assurance that things would be the same as before he left. Well, they weren't going to be, at any rate until she knew a great deal more about the affair. She tried to speak but found that at first she only made a sort of croaking noise.

'Have one of these,' said Graham, holding out a tin of cough pastilles. This made her more angry still, so angry in fact that she found herself quite unable to say anything. Eventually with a great effort she relaxed and managed to say, rather faintly: 'It can't be.'

'What's the matter, darling?' said Graham. 'Sorry to have given you such a fright but, as I said, there's a strike on at the works. So there's nothing for us to do at the office except to wait until it stops. So I thought I'd come home. I'm not all that early, as a matter of fact.'

As Harriet still said nothing and simply looked at him Graham went on: 'Have you been under the weather, darling?'

Harriet could only say: 'I can't believe it.'

'What do you mean?' said Graham. 'There's nothing so odd about it. As a matter of fact, what happened is this. It's not a strike for more pay. The foreman wants to be known as the manager. I said to him, "When I engaged you I engaged you as foreman." He said, "Now look here, Mr Hunt, it may be – " '

But Harriet interrupted at that stage. 'For God's sake stop it.' She walked up to him, and took his arm in one of her hands. 'You're real,' she said.

'I don't understand,' said Graham. 'Just because I come home early one day, there's no need to make a thing of it. You'll be calling it incompatibility next and ask for a divorce.'

'My God!' said Harriet.

Graham put his book down and got up and put his arm round her. 'What is the matter, darling? Let's have a little drink and you'll be all right. I didn't know I'd give you such a shock. I'm dying of thirst. From the way you're behaving you might have been expecting a lover.'

Immediately Harriet looked at her watch. There was still a couple of hours before George was due, she thought. Graham's mouth broke into a smile.

'Don't tell me you are,' he said. 'And after twenty years.'

When he saw that Harriet was not smiling, 'I didn't mean it, darling,' he added. 'I can't think why you seem to be so upset.'

'Graham,' said Harriet, 'are you in your right mind?'

'Me?' said Graham. 'It's you who are behaving as though you weren't. I thought you might be pleased to have me at home early for once. We shall be able to listen to the afternoon Third Programme or something. Oh, I forgot. At least I didn't. Here they are.'

He walked across to the table where there was a Woolworth's bag and took out from it a packet of digestive biscuits. 'There,' he said, triumphantly, putting them on the table. 'And they are McVitie's.'

'What on earth are these?' said Harriet.

'Digestive biscuits,' said Graham. 'You're behaving very oddly. You asked me not to forget and I didn't. When I produce them, you look as though you'd seen a ghost. These are real live digestive biscuits and they come, not from the halls of the mountain king but from that nice little shop where they have that excellent cheese. Now don't tell me you asked me to get half a pound of cheese and I've forgotten it. I'm sure you didn't.'

He paused for a moment or two and then added: 'Well, did you?'

Harriet didn't answer but still looked at him.

'Well, did you?' he repeated. 'I think it was jolly good of me to remember the biscuits. After all, we had quite a trying time with the strike suddenly coming on our hands and I managed to remember it. I'm sure I'd have remembered the cheese too if you'd asked me for it. The association of ideas. I love digestive biscuits and cheese. Do tell me I haven't forgotten.'

Harriet, white-faced, in a very controlled voice but as though it were not really herself speaking, said: 'Graham, darling, you must forgive me for not remembering that I asked you to bring the digestive biscuits.'

Graham interrupted with: 'You did make rather a point of it.' A still very controlled Harriet went on: 'Perhaps I did, Graham, but that was seven years ago.'

The 'seven years' took a second or two to reach Graham's mind. So be began: 'Well, of course, we can't always remember – ', then he added: 'What did you say?'

'You left this house seven years ago,' said Harriet, 'and you've just come back – with a packet of digestive biscuits. Have you had them all the time?'

'What are you talking about?' said Graham. He picked up the packet, opened it and took out a biscuit and ate a piece. 'They're perfectly fresh,' he said. 'Try one yourself. You're talking rubbish.'

Almost like an automaton Harriet took a piece of biscuit herself and ate it. 'Yes,' she said, 'they're perfectly fresh.'

'They're rather nice, as a matter of fact,' said Graham. 'What about a glass of sherry with them?'

The mention of alcohol brought Harriet out of her automatism. She needed some badly. 'How right you are,' she said, 'but it's a large whisky for me.'

She almost ran to the drinks cupboard, poured herself out a large whisky and swallowed it. Meanwhile, Graham was holding out his hand for the glass of sherry which he thought she had gone to get him. Harriet ignored the outstretched hand, poured herself out another large glass of whisky and was about to drink it when she noticed Graham's hand. She put down her glass, poured out a small sherry and took it over to him.

'That's more like you,' said Graham, and lifting up the glass of sherry he sipped it. 'Cheers,' he said. Harriet went back to her own drink and drank it again hurriedly. 'Now let's talk sense,' said Graham. 'What's the matter with you? Aren't you feeling well? Shall I ring Dr Peebles?'

'Dr Peebles,' said Harriet, 'died three years ago.'

'That's very odd,' said Graham. 'D'you remember the last thing I said to him? "Physician, heal thyself." Well, he clearly didn't. But did you say three years? You're talking rubbish again. He was perfectly well three weeks ago when I saw him about that leg of mine.'

'Dr Peebles,' repeated Harriet, 'has been dead for three years. Ring him up if you don't believe me.'

'What's his number?'

'I mean ring up his successor Dr Bulmer.'

'That young man,' said Graham. 'He's only an assistant.'

'He took over the practice three years ago,' said Harriet, 'and you haven't seen him for seven years.'

'Nonsense,' said Graham. 'I can prove it.' He got out his diary and eventually found the page that he was looking for. 'Here it is. Look. "Dr Peebles". And actually three weeks ago. Who says my memory isn't what it was? Actually to the day. Look.'

Harriet looked at the diary for a moment or two and then handed it back to him. 'Have a look at the top of the page, Graham,' she said. 'What does it say there?'

'January, d'you mean?' asked Graham.

'What *year* does it say?'

'What extraordinary questions you're asking,' said Graham. 'This year of course.'

'What is this year?'

'1969, of course.'

Harriet sat down. 'Oh my God,' she said, and after a few seconds she went on. 'Where have you been, Graham?'

'At the office. I told you.'

Harriet looked at him. It certainly appeared that he thought he was speaking the truth. 'Now, Graham,' she went on, 'I'm afraid this is going to be a great shock to you. Drink up your sherry.' Graham drank it.

'Very nice,' he said.

'Then have another,' she said. She poured him out another drink and gave it to him. She poured herself out another whisky and drank it off.

'It's too good to gulp down,' said Graham, and sipped his.

'Now hold my hand, darling,' she said. Graham took her hand.

'I'll come home early again if I'm going to get this sort of treatment,' he said. 'Have you made the bed yet? Of course you have. Let's use the spare room.'

Harriet ignored these remarks and still holding his hand said: 'Graham, your diary says "1969".'

'Of course it does. That's one of the advantages of having a diary.'

'It is now 1976.'

'Don't be silly,' said Graham. 'You've been looking at some stupid TV programme. Where's the paper?'

'I'll get it,' said Harriet. She looked around and eventually found a copy of *The Times*. 'Now hold my hand again,' she said, 'because you're really going to get a shock.'

'Well,' said Graham, 'I can't look at the paper and hold your hand so I'll come back to you in a moment.' He picked up the paper. 'Well, what about it?' he began. 'This is *The Times* all right – oh my God!' he added, and dropped the paper on the floor. 'I think I'd like to hold your hand again,' he said. She took his hand and they both sat down on the sofa. There was complete silence for a few moments and eventually he spoke.

'What on earth has happened?' he said. 'I feel perfectly ordinary. What's been the matter with me? Where have I come from? How did you manage? Why did I go away? Where did I go away?'

'Let's start at the beginning,' said Harriet.

'As far as I'm concerned,' said Graham, 'there isn't any beginning. I left home in the usual way, as I thought, and now I've just come back – with the digestive biscuits.'

'Then let's start at the end,' said Harriet. 'Where did you come from today?'

'I told you. From the office.'

'You can't have,' said Harriet, 'They'd have telephoned at once. You've just come from nowhere and walked straight through that front door.'

'As a matter of fact, I didn't,' said Graham. 'That was funny, come to think of it. You've changed the lock, and the key didn't fit, but fortunately I found the window open in the sitting room so I climbed through.'

'Oh yes,' said Harriet, 'I'd forgotten. I broke my key in it a few years ago.'

'That's all there is to it,' said Graham. 'I went to the office as usual and there was a strike, as I told you, so I came home early. By the way you must have had this chair resprung. Have you missed me?'

'Of course I've missed you.'

'Very much?'

'Of course. Have you missed me?'

'Of course not,' said Graham. 'I didn't know you weren't there. I must have been unconscious for seven years.'

'You look remarkably well on it,' said Harriet, 'though perhaps a bit thinner.'

'I feel extremely well,' said Graham, 'but where have I been? That's what I'd like to know.'

'So would I.'

'You're not suggesting I ran off with some other woman?'

'You can't say you haven't,' said Harriet.

'Of course I haven't.'

'How can you know? During the last seven years you may have been in the arms of sixty women for aught you know.'

'I'm sure I should have remembered that,' said Graham. 'But you say I just went out one morning seven years ago and never came back.'

'That's right.'

'What did you do?'

'First of all I telephoned the office but everyone had gone home. Then I rang one or two of your friends and then I thought there must have been an accident and you'd been knocked down so I got hold of the police.'

'What did they say?'

'They made enquiries of all the hospitals and you weren't in any of them.'

'How could they be sure? I might have been unconscious. How could they tell that every man who was brought into hospital on that day wasn't me?'

'Of course they couldn't tell at the time but the next day I showed them your photo, they duplicated it and sent it round to all the hospitals.'

'And I wasn't there?'

'So they said.'

'And where was I?'

'I've told you. That's what I want to know.'

'What sort of clothes was I wearing?'

'How can I remember that? But let's look inside the pocket of your jacket and see what it says.'

They looked inside the inner pocket of his coat.

'7-4-67, it says,' said Graham. 'It's probably the suit I went away in. Don't you remember it?'

'Now you mention it,' said Harriet, 'I do. But it's worn remarkably well. You can't have been wearing this one suit for seven years.'

'D'you think I must have changed from time to time?'

'It wouldn't have this nap on it if you hadn't.'

'I've always been very careful with my clothes,' said Graham, 'as you know.'

'Let's look at the seat of the trousers,' said Harriet. 'Get up and show me.' He got up and exhibited his behind to her.

'They're hardly shiny at all,' said Harriet. 'That seat of yours hasn't been sitting in those trousers for seven whole years on end.'

'I must have gone to bed from time to time.'

'I expect you did.'

'But how did you manage when I didn't come back? Don't tell me you had to go out to work.'

'No. After you'd been away a month I received a cheque from a firm of solicitors in Birmingham for a hundred pounds. Of course I asked who had told them to send it and they refused to tell me. They said they'd be sending a hundred pounds a month. I told the police about that and they went to see the solicitor, but he said that he couldn't disclose who his client was.'

'How long did the payments go on for?'

'They're still going on as far as I know. I had the last cheque last month. Oh good Lord!' she said suddenly. She had only just remembered that that morning she had divorced Graham. 'Graham, darling, I'm sorry but you're not going to like this. This morning I tried to divorce you for being dead.'

'But I'm not.'

'The judge said he wasn't satisfied that you were but he gave me a divorce on the grounds of desertion.'

'But I don't understand these hundred pounds a month. I haven't been giving anybody a hundred pounds a month.'

'My counsel suggested that you might have given a lump sum in the first instance.'

'A hundred pounds a month for seven years. That would amount to eight or nine thousand pounds. Where should I get that from unless I cashed my insurance policy?'

'As a matter of fact,' said Harriet, 'I was trying to get that insurance money, but I could only get it if you were dead. The bank said they still had the policy, so you couldn't have paid it out of that.'

'Well, I hadn't any money under the bed,' said Graham, 'or anywhere else.'

'How did you get the hundred pounds a month?'

'I've no idea. But how do you know it was I who was sending the hundred pounds a month?'

'Who else could it have been? Of course it was you. And I don't mind telling you that I was hopping mad when I had the first cheque.'

'Not enough?' asked Graham.

'Well, it isn't now. But that isn't the point. You left me after twenty years without a word and then pensioned me off with a hundred pounds a month. Naturally I was livid. I still don't know that this isn't what happened and that you haven't been spending the last seven years with a girlfriend.'

'I wouldn't have dreamt of doing such a thing,' said Graham. 'Why should I? I couldn't have been happy with anyone except you.'

'So you say. But neither of us can know that it's the truth.'

'Anyway, what did you want to divorce me for?'

'Really!' said Harriet. 'If you leave a wife without a word for seven years, what do you expect her to do? I was lonely.'

'Were you going to marry someone else?'

'Not immediately.'

'Who?'

'I said "not immediately".'

'But if it had been immediately, who would it have been?'

'George.'

'Not George Pennyfeather or whatever his name was?'

'Pennypacker.'

'That's just as bad. What d'you want to marry him for?'

'He asked me.'

'You didn't have to agree.'

'I was lonely.'

'Did you never think of me? I was lonely too. And anyway, this George Pennyfarthing. Have you been living with him?'

'No,' said Harriet. 'But I'd like to know how you've been living.'

'As far as I know,' said Graham, 'I've been living a completely blameless life.'

'But you don't know how you've been living.'

'Tell me frankly,' said Graham. 'Do you think it would have been completely in character for me to go away with someone else without saying a word to you? And then suddenly come back after seven years?'

'No, I don't think it would be in character. But apart from not knowing whether you went away with someone else, it's what you've done. And you sent me a hundred pounds a month.'

'You can't know for certain that I sent it,' said Graham.

'Of course I can. Who else can possibly have sent it?'

'George,' said Graham.

53

'Don't be ridiculous,' said Harriet. 'The first payment came a month after you'd left. I hadn't taken up with him then.'

'Oh, you hadn't taken up with him then,' repeated Graham. 'Since when have you taken up with him?'

'Over the years,' said Harriet, 'naturally I've seen more and more of him. You can't blame me for that.'

'Well, there's no accounting for tastes,' said Graham. 'I never could stick the fellow personally.'

'You used to play golf with him,' said Harriet.

'I could beat him.'

'Tell me something else,' said Harriet. 'You used to go away for your firm quite often. Where did you go?'

'I must have told you at the time. Various places.'

'Such as?'

'Torquay, Llandudno, Keswick.'

'What did you go to Keswick for?'

'Business, of course. You aren't suggesting that these trips of mine are anything to do with my loss of memory, are you? For one thing I always phoned you wherever I was.'

'That's true.'

'Have you ever known me lie to you?' said Graham. 'On anything serious, I mean.'

'I can't say that I have,' said Harriet. 'But we've got to try and sort this thing out. George is coming to dinner tonight.'

'Put him off. You don't want him now that I'm back, do you?'

'I don't know what I want,' said Harriet. 'If what you tell me is true and you really lost your memory for seven years, you'll have to see a doctor. It's a very serious matter. After all, if it happened once it could happen again. Apart from that, what have you done during those seven years? You may have married somebody else for aught I know. You may have had children – anything. I've read of cases where a man has lost his memory for a few hours or even a few days but never as much as seven years or anything like it. It's quite appalling. Have you been in England all the time?'

'I don't actually remember going abroad,' said Graham.

'But you don't remember anything. So you may have been in the United States of America all the time. Have you got a passport on you?'

Graham searched through his pockets but found nothing of interest.

'Let's look at everything you've got,' said Harriet.

First of all Graham took the money out of his trouser pocket. There were two half crowns, a shilling and five old pennies.

'They're no good,' said Harriet, 'except for the shilling. We've gone decimal since you went away.'

'What d'you mean?'

Harriet explained. Graham then took out his pocket book and emptied its contents. He also took out his diary and they looked through it together. Everything related to the year in which he disappeared, 1969.

'It's extraordinary,' he said. 'How have I been living? Have I opened another banking account? Good gracious,' he added, 'I may be a millionaire for all I know. Perhaps I've won a football pool.'

'You may be a millionaire,' said Harriet, 'but how are we going to live? I bet the hundred pounds a month will stop now, and, even if it didn't, it's nothing like enough. If you have any money, where do you keep it and how are we going to find it? Perhaps if you have some psychoanalysis we'll be able to discover more about you.'

'We'll have to try, I agree,' said Graham. 'In the meantime, do put your George off. You don't want him now surely? Are you fond of him?'

'Well,' said Harriet, 'when you didn't come back I thought you must have gone off with somebody else and I did become fond of George eventually. It was only natural. He was very kind to me. It's all very well for you to turn up as though nothing had happened. It may not have happened from your point of view but a lot has happened from mine.'

'The law can't be such an ass as all that,' said Graham. 'If I go to the court and say that I'm here they'll cancel the order surely?'

'I suppose they might,' said Harriet.

'Suppose?' said Graham. 'Don't you want them to?' He paused for a moment and then he said: 'Really darling, if you want to keep your divorce and if you want to marry George, I won't stand in your way. I'll go away again if you really want me to. There's no point in my living with you if you want to be living with somebody else. But I couldn't marry again myself. I was always a one woman man. I say, what's that?' he said, looking at the table where he had laid out the things from his pockets. It was an old letter. He picked it up. 'Good God! This is a letter from you. I must read it.' He started to do so. 'It's really rather nice. It's a lovely letter. The first time we were away from each other after we were married. Good Lord! D'you see what you said?' He showed her the passage. 'That makes me feel quite young again.'

Harriet looked at the letter and then suddenly burst into tears. Graham put his arm around her.

'Don't worry, darling. We'll sort this thing out. And if you still don't feel like you said in the letter about me after we've been together for twenty-four hours or so, I'll leave you to George Pennyfeather without a word. I must say I hope you won't. Pretty awful to go out one morning leaving my loving wife behind me and to come back in the evening a few hours later to find that she wants to live with another man.'

Harriet blew her nose and wiped away her tears. 'Sorry, darling,' she said. 'I can see it from your point of view but I am sure you can see it from mine. What's the first thing you remember about today?'

'Today? Well, I went to the office.'

'You didn't, you know,' said Harriet, but you think you did. You think you remember it.'

'I'm sure I did,' said Graham. 'And then there was this strike – now you mention it, it is a little blurred. But one thing I certainly remember and that's buying digestive biscuits.'

'Where did you buy them?'

'In Redgrave. The little shop at the corner of the High Street. I remember passing Woolworth's and deciding to give the little shop the chance.'

'That little shop,' said Harriet, 'gave up business two years ago.'

'I certainly bought the biscuits.'

'That's true,' said Harriet. 'Let's look at the bag.' She picked it up. 'This is a Woolworth's bag,' she said.

Graham looked at it, 'I could have sworn,' he said, 'but you're quite right. It is a Woolworth's bag. I'm sorry about that little shop. I've often wondered how they'd manage to get through. Apparently they didn't.'

Harriet looked through some of the documents on the table. 'You know you haven't had those in your pockets all the time. You can't have gone about like this for several years. What must have happened is that you've been wearing other clothes, you've had other documents and all sorts of things in the last seven years. And now to come home you've put on this suit.'

Harriet stopped for a moment or two. She suddenly began to wonder whether the whole thing was a bit of play-acting. If Graham had been off with another woman and eventually got tired of her and decided to come back, to avoid awkward questions he might have pretended to have lost his memory. Admittedly it appeared very genuine and his reactions to everything were what you would have expected of a man who had just come back from the unremembered. But that such cases were very rare indeed she felt sure.

'Graham,' she said eventually, 'are you leading me up the garden?'

'Leading you up the garden? What do you mean?'

'You know perfectly well what I mean. Are you just pretending to have lost your memory and in fact do you know perfectly well what's happened during the last seven years.'

'Why on earth should I do a thing like that?'

'There's a simple answer to that,' said Harriet. 'If you haven't lost your memory you've got seven years in your life to account for. You may have got married. You're not the sort of person to commit bigamy but, if you thought you would get away with it with me, you may have thought you could get away with it with her.'

'I don't like this "get away with it". If you think I'm telling you a pack of lies for Heaven's sake just say so. It would be so much easier.'

'Why?' said Harriet. 'Why would it be so much easier if I tell you I don't believe you?'

'At least I'd know what I'm up against,' said Graham.

'D'you remember going to those solicitors in Birmingham, Pettifer & Jones?' asked Harriet.

'Pettifer & Jones? Pettifer & Jones? Never heard of them. I know. Let's ring them up. They may be able to help. Let's see their last letter and we'll ring them at once.'

'That's a very good idea.' Harriet went to a drawer and opened it and brought out a letter. 'Here we are,' she said. 'I'll ring them. Stupid of us really not to think of it before.' She went to the telephone and dialled the necessary number. 'They'll be able to solve the whole thing. Who shall I ask for?'

'I suggest you ask for the person who signed the letter. Let me have a look.' He picked up the letter. 'JP. That's easy. John Pettifer.'

'He was the man who gave evidence this morning,' said Harriet. 'He may not be back in his office.'

'Tell me what he said,' said Graham. Harriet told him. 'Well, that doesn't help very much,' said Graham. 'He's never seen me himself, if it was me. However, I think it's worth while ringing them and see what they can tell us.'

By this time Pettifer & Jones had answered.

'My name is Mrs Hunt,' said Harriet. 'I'm speaking from The Cottage, London Lane, near Redgrave. Could I speak to Mr John Pettifer, please? He gave evidence in my case this morning. As a matter of fact I want him to speak to my husband.'

'Your husband?' said the girl in Pettifer & Jones' office in a tone of surprise. 'Your husband?'

She was Mr Pettifer's secretary and knew all about the case.

'That's right,' said Harriet. 'I found him here when I got back.'

'Good gracious!' said the girl. 'Mr Pettifer will be surprised. I'll fetch him.'

There was a delay of a minute or so and then Mr Pettifer came to the telephone. 'Is that Mrs Hunt?'

'Yes.'

'My secretary tells me that your husband has just returned.'

'That's right.'

'But that's extraordinary. Where has he been all this time?'

'That's why I'm ringing you,' said Harriet. 'He says he doesn't know.'

'Doesn't know?'

'Let me speak to him,' said Graham, and he took the receiver from Harriet. 'Hullo?' he said. 'Is that Mr Pettifer? I understand that your firm has been sending my wife a hundred pounds a month. I'd be glad to know who gave you instructions to do this. Of course I understand it's confidential, but, as my wife seems to think that I gave you the instructions, I can authorise you to tell me all about it.'

'If,' said Mr Pettifer, 'you are the person who gave me the instructions, that's quite true. But how am I to know? I don't know your voice.'

'I am Graham Hunt,' said Graham. 'My wife can confirm it to you if you want. But you didn't see the man who gave you the instructions. Who did?'

'The man is dead, I'm afraid.'

'But the notes he made must be available,' said Graham. 'What do they say?'

'How can I tell you that,' said Mr Pettifer, 'without being quite certain that you are the person who gave the instructions?'

'Well, who else could have given them to you?' asked Graham.

'Quite theoretically,' said Mr Pettifer uneasily, 'quite theoretically it could have been someone who had the interests of your wife at heart.'

'In the particular circumstances of this case,' said Graham, 'who could that have been but me? You are not, I hope, suggesting that my wife was having an affair with another man.'

'Of course not,' said Mr Pettifer.

'Are you quite sure of that?' asked Graham.

'Really, Mr Hunt,' said Mr Pettifer, 'you're putting me in very great difficulty. How can I be sure of anything? Please understand I'm not making the slightest suggestion against your wife but I can only speak of things of which I know and in fact I know nothing in this case, except that my firm was given money to pay on and we have paid on what we were told to pay on. That is precisely all I know. The money may have come from a godfather or a relative or – '

'Or a lover,' put in Graham.

'Well, you said it, Mr Hunt,' said Mr Pettifer, 'but let me make it plain that personally I don't believe it was from anybody except you.'

'If you believe it to have been from me,' said Graham, 'why can't you give me the information for which I was asking? Did I give you the money in a lump sum or have I been sending the money each month? Or several times a year or something of that sort? Why on earth can't you tell me the facts now that you know that I'm alive and well?'

'I'm extremely sorry not to be more helpful,' said Pettifer. 'The judge at the trial said that I was quite entitled to withhold the information. I suggest that the best thing is for you to go to another solicitor and let him communicate with me. It may be that we shall be able to sort things out.'

'All right,' said Graham, 'I'll do that. Thank you very much. Goodbye.' And he put down the receiver. 'Well, I didn't get any change out of him,' he said. 'These lawyers are the end. So you got a divorce from me on the ground that I left you.'

'Yes.'

'We can soon put that right. You only got it today. But what troubles me now, darling, is that you seem to think that this was all part of a hoax. We were very happy together, weren't we, darling.'

'Yes, we were.'

'Why can't we be happy again? I can't really blame you, I suppose. There are two possibilities. One is that I am telling you a cock and bull story, that I walked off with another woman or something of that sort and then, when she turned me out or I got tired of her, came back to you and pretended that I had lost my memory. That's one possibility. The other is that I really did lose my memory and somehow or other made another life for myself somewhere else. And suddenly my memory came back and at the same time I lost the memory of all the things I've done during the last seven years. Which of those two stories is the more likely?'

'You put it very well,' said Harriet. 'If it were anybody but you I would have said the first.'

'You're quite right, darling,' said Graham. 'So would I. We know that there are such things as loss of memory but usually it happens when it's convenient for the memory to be lost. A man kills somebody and says he's had a blackout. A soldier walks out of the firing line and says he doesn't remember it. A person is charged with shoplifting and says she's no recollection of anything that happened.'

'Why she and not he?' asked Harriet.

'All right then. Let it pass. But it is a known fact that this sort of amnesia does very occasionally occur.'

'How on earth did you get the money to live on, let alone send me a hundred pounds a month?'

'That's what I should like to know,' said Graham. 'If I've been using a different name, I may have got banking accounts in that name. I wonder what I'm worth? I may be a millionaire. I might have won half a dozen football pools or premium bonds. I may have got thousands of pounds in a safe deposit or a lot of gold and silver or other valuables. How do we find out? The trouble is that, even if we employ detectives to infiltrate into Pettifer & Jones and see exactly what did happen, I don't believe they'd be able to find out anything. I think in fact they've completely lost track of their client and that in their files there will be no information at all except that a man who said his name was such and such came in and instructed them to send the money to you every month. Either he gave them a lump sum or he kept on sending more.'

'Presumably he had an address,' said Harriet. 'We might learn something from that.'

'I should have thought that we needn't spend hundreds of pounds on detectives to find out that sort of information. Another firm of solicitors ought to be able to get it in the end somehow. Now that I've returned, I mean, I'm really the only person who could have done it. How on earth did I earn it and where?'

'I wish I could believe you,' said Harriet. Then she added, 'The only thing is – '

'The only thing is what?' asked Graham.

'It's a pretty unpleasant choice. If you're telling me the truth, you must have been insane or the equivalent for seven years. And that means that I've got a husband who is liable to do the same thing again.'

'What a horrible thought,' said Graham.

'That's perfectly true,' said Harriet. 'That's one alternative. You'll have to be psychiatrised or psychoanalysed or I don't know what else. The other alternative is what I said before. That you're a bloody liar and leading me up the garden. You admitted yourself that that's much more likely.'

'Which would you prefer to be the case?' asked Graham.

'Then you have been putting on an act?'

'Good gracious no! I just wondered which would be the better for you. I can see that it must be pretty awful for you to have an invalid on your hands for the rest of your life, because I suppose that's what I am. I'm all right physically and from my point of view I'm all right mentally. But I can't be if I can lose my memory for seven years. All right, darling,' he said, after a moment. 'If that's too frightening a thought, I'll just disappear again. And this time I'll never come back. You won't mind if I pack a few things first?'

'You haven't got any things,' said Harriet. 'Eventually I gave them all away.'

'That's a blow. Never mind. I'll go as I am. In what I've got on. That's if you want me to.'

'Honestly I don't know what I want. I loved you and I've always wanted you back and, if you'd come back and said what you'd done, I'm pretty certain that I should have forgiven you and we could have started all over again. But to start life again on the basis of a pack of lies – '

Graham interrupted. 'If it *is* a pack of lies, darling.'

'You said yourself that's the probability.'

'I quite agree the probability but not a certainty. I believe you'd really prefer me to tell you that I've been away for seven years with Queenie Hottentot and that, when she left me for somebody else, I came back to you. You would, wouldn't you? What you're saying to yourself is "better to have a bad husband than a mad husband".'

'And,' added Harriet, 'after all a bad husband did live with me very happily for twenty years and he did come back in the end. Yes, I think you're right, darling. Tell me that's what happened. Except that I don't believe her name was Queenie Hottentot.'

'I would, darling, if I could. I really would. It would be so very much easier for one thing. But I can't.'

Was he being very clever, thought Harriet, in refusing to take what appeared to be an easy course, trying to show how genuine he is? Or is he genuine?

Neither of them said anything for a few minutes and then Graham suddenly had a thought. 'I think I'll ring the office,' he said. 'They may be able to help me in some way. I remember the number quite plainly.' He went to the telephone and dialled the number. As soon as it was answered, 'Hullo, hullo,' he said. 'Is that Marjoribanks & Co? Could I speak to Mr Brownjohn, please?'

'I'm afraid Mr Brownjohn has been dead for two years,' said the telephonist at the other end.

'I'm sorry,' said Graham. 'This is Graham Hunt speaking. I don't know if you were in the office seven years ago? No. Well, I quite understand. Um – is Mr Woods there?'

'No, I'm afraid he's left. About eighteen months ago.'

'What about Mr Thornton? Is he still there?'

'He's retired, I'm afraid.'

'D'you think you could find anybody in the office who does remember me? I tell you it's Graham Hunt. I was in the office seven years ago.'

'I'll see if I can find someone,' said the telephonist. 'Graham Hunt, I think you said?'

'That's right.'

'Please hold on.'

'They all seem to be dead or retired,' said Graham.

A little while later another voice came on the line. 'My name is Morgan, Mr Hunt. I just remember you. I had only just come to the office when you left. I was little more than an office boy then. I've got your job now. My name's Morgan, I said.'

'Morgan,' said Graham, reflectively. 'Morgan. Yes, I think I remember you. An extraordinary thing but I appear to have suffered a loss of memory. Perhaps you'd tell the partners, would you, about me? I'll come into the office tomorrow and see what can be arranged.'

'I'm afraid you'll find a lot of changes,' said Morgan. 'We've been taken over by Whitstable & Company.'

'Whitstable & Company?' said Graham. 'Never heard of them. I suppose I'd better come along. There are some loose ends to clear up. After all, if you've got my job you must know it's a pretty important one. Oh, don't worry, I shan't try and do you out of it. It may be someone in the office will be able to help. Thank you very much indeed. Goodbye.'

After he'd replaced the receiver Graham said: 'I bet he's saying "If he thinks he's going to pinch my job, he's got another think coming." I don't altogether blame him.'

'What are you going to do?' asked Harriet. 'I'm sure they won't want you back there. A man who's lost his memory for seven years wouldn't exactly be an asset.'

'It isn't going to be easy, is it?' said Graham. 'What's the state of the employment market at the moment?'

'Very bad. You'll find it extremely difficult to get another job. You'll probably have to accept social security.'

'I don't see why I shouldn't,' said Graham. 'I've paid in long enough and never had anything out. But what does it cost to live these days?'

'I've just about been able to manage,' said Harriet. 'I had twenty-five pounds a week from you and Uncle Arthur died and left me two thousand pounds. That was a tremendous help. I've sold a few things and, you'll never guess, I earned two hundred pounds in three weeks. How d'you think I did it?'

'I'm a bit out of things,' said Graham. 'You tell me.'

'Shelling peas.'

'Shelling peas! Shelling peas!'

'The hours were long but it was only for three weeks. It was well worth it. As a matter of fact you've come back just at the right time.'

'That's the nicest thing you've said since I came,' said Graham. 'Let's have another drink. I'll do it this time. See if I remember. What're you going to have?'

'Whisky, I think, please.'

Graham poured out a large whisky for Harriet and took a sherry for himself. 'How much is whisky, by the way? I suppose it's gone up?'

'You're going to have another shock,' said Harriet, 'if your story's true. I should sit down. A bottle of whisky will now cost you about three pounds fifty.'

'What d'you mean?' said Graham. 'Fifty?'

'Oh good Lord,' said Harriet. 'We've gone decimal now. There are a hundred pennies in a pound so three pounds fifty is the equivalent of what used to be called three pounds ten.'

'Three pounds ten for a bottle of whisky!' exclaimed Graham. 'I'm not surprised you don't find twenty-five pounds a week enough to live on. But that's quite appalling. Wages have gone up, I imagine, too.'

'You're right,' said Harriet. 'D'you know that a typist who can't do forty words a minute and who can't do shorthand and who can't spell can easily earn thirty or forty pounds a week now. While really first-class secretaries are almost unobtainable and can earn five thousand a year.'

'I wonder what my salary would have been now,' said Graham, 'I was getting about three thousand five hundred and it should be at least double that. I ought to have asked Morgan when I was speaking to him on the phone, but I suppose it might have been embarrassing for him. You'd better tell me something about your relations. How's that awful brother-in-law of yours?'

'You'll be glad to hear he's gone to Australia.'

'Oh Lord, then I suppose you'll be ringing up your sister there. That'll cost a packet.'

'I do ring her occasionally but d'you know it's so clear it might be next door.'

'That's a pity,' said Graham. 'That'll encourage you.'

'On the other hand, twenty-five pounds a week discouraged me very considerably.'

'We'll imagine that's all you're going to get now I'm back. I wonder how long that hundred pounds a month will go on for? I imagine it must stop now that I shan't be paying any more to the solicitors.'

'Unless you gave them a lump sum.'

'How on earth could I have done that? I've never had ten thousand pounds in cash in my life. My only substantial asset was the insurance policy.'

'I don't know what we're going to do,' said Harriet. 'If you're telling me the truth you must have been and may still be a very sick man.'

'I feel fine,' said Graham. 'If you'll come to bed now to celebrate my return, I'll prove it to you. But hadn't you better ring up George and put him off? It might be awkward if he came back in the middle.'

While they were talking, Graham was looking through the bits and pieces of paper which had come out of his pocket. 'I say, look at this,' he said suddenly. He held up two stubs of theatre tickets. 'This was the first theatre I ever took you to. I've always kept those stubs.'

'You're a sentimental old fool,' said Harriet.

'Of course I am,' said Graham. 'And look. D'you remember this photograph? I took it on our honeymoon.' He showed it to her. 'You've hardly changed a bit. Even your hair's the same colour.'

'Well – ' began Harriet but she did not complete the sentence.

'Mine isn't, I suppose,' said Graham.

'Well,' said Harriet, 'it is a little bit grey.'

'Odd,' said Graham, 'to go out with brown hair in the morning and come back with it grey in the afternoon. That's a detail,' he went on. 'What are we going to do about George? Better ring him up and put him off, hadn't you? How will he take it?'

'He won't like it at all,' said Harriet, 'if I say that I'm going back to you.'

'What d'you mean? Going back to me. You're still with me. You never left me.'

'You left me,' said Harriet.

'Not intentionally,' said Graham. 'You do believe that, don't you, now.'

Harriet hesitated. 'I'm not sure, but I suppose I do. I don't think you're that sort of man. You never did like a change. I can't see you suddenly buzzing off with Sarah Wilcox.'

'Who the devil's she?'

'Don't you remember? You told me that she was the most beautiful girl you'd ever seen.'

'Did I really? Then she must have been. I don't lie to you on serious matters.'

'And perhaps this may help to bring it to your mind,' said Harriet. 'You said it on my birthday.'

'That doesn't sound like me,' said Graham. 'Perhaps it was George or some other man you met during the last seven years.'

'It was you,' said Harriet, 'and you said it on my birthday.'

'How well did I know the girl?'

'As a matter of fact you only met her once at dinner. I only quoted her as an example. No, if it had been anybody else, I don't think I'd have believed your story.'

'If it had been George, for instance?'

'No,' said Harriet, 'I don't think I'd have believed it of George.'

'Who would you have believed it of except me?'

'Well,' said Harriet, 'the Archbishop of Canterbury, I suppose. Or Lord Longford.'

'I wonder if other people would believe it. After all most people don't know me as you do. I don't think I'd believe it myself if somebody else told it to me. That awful brother of yours, for example.'

At that moment there was a ring at the bell. Harriet went to the door and opened it. She found waiting outside a small woman of about forty-five. She had sharpish features and, when she spoke, she sounded as though she were out of breath although she wasn't.

'Oh good morning,' she said. 'I'm so sorry to trouble you but I believe Mr Simpkins lives here.'

'Simpkins?' said Harriet. 'No, certainly not. My name is Hunt.'

'But surely,' said the woman, 'this is the right address. This is The Cottage, London Lane?'

'That's right,' said Harriet. 'The previous owner's name was Wellerby and we've been here for many years.'

'And your name is Hunt, is it? Is your husband by any chance in?'

Harriet paused for a moment, then 'Yes,' she said, 'he is.'

'I wonder if I might see him?'

'Can you tell me what it's about?'

'I come from the CPA.'

'CPA?' queried Harriet. 'Carter Paterson Associates, is it? Has there been misdelivery of a parcel or something?'

'No,' said the woman. 'CPA. Citizens' Protection Association. My name is Rosemary Clinch and I'm one of the executives.'

'Why should you want to protect my husband?'

'I don't.'

'Then may I ask what you do want?'

'Ah,' said Miss Clinch, 'I would want to protect him if he were Mr Simpkins. As he's Mr Hunt, he doesn't come into it.'

'Then why do you want to see him?'

'Just in case Mr Hunt is Mr Simpkins,' said Miss Clinch.

'You'd better come in, Miss Clinch,' said Harriet.

As soon as Miss Clinch came into the room she saw Graham. She smiled and then went straight forward to him with outstretched hand. 'How nice to meet you again, Mr Simpkins,' she said.

CHAPTER SIX

The CPA

The CPA had been founded by Archibald Hardcross who, until the events which preceded its foundation, had been a firm believer in British justice. He was by no means a complete fool and he knew that no system of justice could be perfect, and that lawyers and juries and even judges were liable to make mistakes. After all they were only human. But at the same time he believed wholeheartedly in British justice and, as far as he was concerned, if a jury said that a man was guilty of a serious offence, he believed the convicted man to have been as guilty as if he had seen him commit the crime himself. Whenever a criminal case caused a lot of public interest and the person charged with the crime was convicted or acquitted Archibald could be heard in his club or in the theatre during an interval holding forth on the correctness of the jury's verdict. 'They used to be twelve good men and true,' he would say, 'and now they are twelve good men and women and true, and none the worse for the addition of the weaker sex. I have been on a jury myself and I know that in the days of the death penalty it was with a very heavy heart indeed that a jury would bring in a verdict of guilty. But you can be quite sure that, if that was their verdict, that was the truth of the matter.'

'Has there never been a miscarriage of justice in your view?' an enquirer would ask.

'None that I know of,' he would say.

'What about Beck and Slater?'

'They were a long time ago,' he would say, 'and none of us know all the facts. But I wouldn't be too sure that either of them was innocent.'

When it was pointed out to him that partly as a result of the Beck case Parliament introduced the Court of Criminal Appeal he said: 'So what? I've nothing against the Court of Criminal Appeal. The fact that Parliament thought that there might be a risk of innocent men being convicted is no reason whatever for saying that they have been. Plenty of guilty men have been acquitted and I don't complain of that. It is indeed better that ninety-nine guilty men should be acquitted than that one innocent man should be convicted. I'm only talking of serious crime, not of motoring and other petty offences. But when a jury, after being directed by a judge comes to the unanimous conclusion that a man is guilty, in my view there's no doubt whatever about it.'

'But we have majority verdicts now,' someone would say. 'What do you say to them?'

'Quite frankly,' said Archibald, 'I don't like them. And I would agree with you that, if there were a majority of ten to two and there appeared to be uncertainties in the case, I personally would not be satisfied with that verdict. Indeed, when the question of majority verdicts was being canvassed in Parliament, I wrote a letter to *The Times* stating as strongly as I could that in my view there should be no change in a system which had worked well for hundreds of years. Unfortunately Parliament didn't agree with me and now we have majority verdicts. I'm not talking of such cases. What I am saying is that, when a jury unanimously decides that a man or woman is guilty and no mistake in law has been made by the judge, that verdict should be upheld.'

'What about the Wallace case?' someone asked. 'No mistake in law was made by the judge, the jury convicted him and the Court of Criminal Appeal said the verdict was an unreasonable one and upset it.'

'Well,' said Archibald, 'the jury saw Wallace and the other witnesses and they were satisfied of his guilt. I'm not a lawyer and I'm not saying that the Court was wrong to do what it did. But if you ask me to go further than that and say that I believe in Mr Wallace's innocence, quite frankly I don't. I'll tell you something. I'm a rich man and, if I felt that a man had been wrongly convicted of a serious crime, I'd be prepared to put up a lot of money to help such a man to upset the conviction. But my money's safe enough,' he added. 'There aren't any such cases today. There may have been in the past when politics played too great a part in the matter. In the days of Judge Jeffreys for example, or earlier than that. I wouldn't know, but you take it from me that, when the foreman of the jury says guilty of murder or rape or serious violence, theft or fraud, the chap did it.'

This then was Archibald Hardcross' standpoint for many years, until one day he received a great shock. A man who was suspected of a serious robbery was detained by a police constable but not for very long, for he hit the police constable so often and so hard that the unfortunate officer remembered nothing until he woke up in hospital. When later the police constable's memory returned, he identified a man called Brighthouse as his assailant. He had no doubt whatever that his identification was correct. Another man, who had seen the police constable knocked down and who went to his assistance, also identified

Brighthouse as the man whom he saw running away from the scene. Brighthouse was sent for trial and in due course he was convicted of assault with intent to cause grievous bodily harm. His defence was that at the time of the assault he was in bed with his wife and he called her to corroborate his evidence. Neither he nor his wife gave their evidence well and the jury found him guilty after retiring for only a quarter of an hour. Brighthouse had several previous convictions for serious offences and the judge sent him to prison for fourteen years. Before he was sentenced Brighthouse said to the judge: 'My Lord, before God and your Lordship I am not guilty of this crime and one day I shall prove it.' One day this was proved and what was proved was not only that Brighthouse did not commit the crime but that he couldn't have committed it. For at the time when the unfortunate officer was being assaulted Brighthouse himself was opening somebody's safe thirty miles away. At his trial for assaulting the police officer he had not unnaturally been somewhat hesitant to put forward the true alibi but, when the Home Secretary went into the matter, it was absolutely plain that Brighthouse was as innocent of the assault on the police officer as was the Home Secretary himself. But the Home Secretary would have had a more attractive alibi.

When the true facts came to the attention of Archibald he was absolutely horrified. Here was a man who had been sentenced to fourteen years' imprisonment for a crime of which he was completely innocent. It wasn't a case of there being some doubt about his guilt. Here was a man who under the system which he had lauded for so many years had been convicted of somebody else's crime. After a few days' unhappiness Archibald proceeded to go into reverse. If such a thing could happen to Brighthouse, it could happen to other people. There was something very wrong. People pointed out to him that the verdict was partly due to Brighthouse's own fault in committing perjury and persuading his wife to commit perjury at his trial. Archibald would have none of it. 'It was for the prosecution to prove its case, wasn't it,' he said, 'and this sort of thing must not happen again. I will start an association for the purpose of preventing it.'

And so the Citizens' Protection Association was born. It is a well-known fact that a convert to a religion is often far more emphatic in stating his beliefs than the believers whom he has just joined. Archibald now started to look for injustice wherever he could see a possibility of its having occurred. He openly invited anybody who considered that he was wrongly convicted to write to him to ask for assistance. He was bombarded with letters. Not in the least dismayed at the amount of work which this might involve he engaged a large staff to assist him. On one occasion owing to his efforts a man who had been convicted of stealing five hundred pounds received a free pardon, and three hundred pounds compensation. The man was aged forty and had eight previous convictions against him for dishonesty. When Archibald boasted about his success at his club a fellow member said to him: 'You say this fellow had eight previous convictions?' 'Yes.' 'How many offences d'you think he committed for which he was never caught?' 'What d'you mean?' asked Archibald. 'Are you suggesting that every time he committed a crime he was found out? said his friend. 'He must have been a pretty regular criminal to have eight previous convictions against him. How many years did he serve in prison in respect of his previous convictions?' 'I haven't added it up,' said Archibald, 'but I should think between ten and fifteen.' 'And how much did he get for this offence for which he was shown to be innocent in the end?' 'Three years, but he only served nine months before he was let out.' 'Why didn't you ask him how much he'd made out of the crimes for which he was never tried?' 'I didn't think it was my place to do that,' said Archibald. 'If he wanted compensation,' said the friend, 'surely the only way to assess it is to draw up a balance sheet. If the man has been convicted eight times you can be pretty certain he's probably committed at least twenty or thirty or many more crimes. Wouldn't it be fairer to the public to ask him – not with a view to further prosecutions but simply in order to see that he was paid the right amount for the nine months he wrongly served – wouldn't it be fairer to ask him how much he'd made out of these other crimes? Suppose it turned out that he'd made three thousand pounds out of crimes for which he'd served no sentence and which were never taken into consideration when he was convicted of any other crime, he'd have got away with three thousand pounds. Now he's served nine months which he shouldn't have served. I should have thought that in a case like that honours were easy.'

'Have you ever been to prison?' asked Archibald.

'Of course not.'

'What d'you think it must be like to be in prison for nine months in respect of a crime you haven't committed?'

'Well, I don't suppose he was very pleased but it wasn't as though prison were a new thing to him. After all, you said yourself he's served about ten to fifteen years, so he knew all about it. It wasn't like the shock that a first offender receives when he first goes inside. When you point to the unpleasantness of him serving nine months for a crime which he hadn't committed, what about the pleasure for him when he had three thousand pounds to play with for crimes which he did commit but which were never brought home to him?'

'How d'you know he got three thousand pounds?'

'Of course I don't. I merely took that as a figure. But I should have thought that every regular criminal, according to his ability, makes quite a lot out of crimes for which he's never even suspected. I grant you that there are some pretty poor performers who only pick up a few pounds here and there. All right. If your man was a performer like that let him say so. Let him show that in the thirty cases of burglary which were never taken into consideration he only made an average of ten pounds a burglary. That would be a total of about three hundred pounds. On that showing when you draw your balance sheet you might say that probably the right figure to give him for nine months was five hundred pounds. Subtract the three hundred and he gets two hundred. If that was the sort of man your client was in the present case I don't complain at three hundred pounds. There isn't much in it. But I'm sure that wasn't the way in which the Home Secretary went about it. You didn't go about it in that way. You'd say you mustn't ask a chap about his past. That's his affair. That isn't British. Well, quite frankly I say poppycock. If a man's been wrongfully convicted he should no doubt be given compensation, but in fixing the amount you must look at both sides of the coin.'

'I can only say,' said Archibald, 'that I profoundly disagree. As a matter of fact I'm on a new line of case altogether now. I'm on fingerprints.'

'What d'you mean you're on fingerprints?'

'Well,' said Archibald, 'for years it has been believed that if a man's fingerprints were on the gun or on the scene of the crime they couldn't lie and he must be guilty. But it has recently been discovered that fingerprints can be removed from one place to another. This can be done either by a corrupt policeman or by somebody who wanted to frame the person in question.'

'What are you doing about it?'

'As a matter of fact there have been quite a number of cases of people who have been convicted mainly on fingerprint evidence. Sometimes they have vehemently denied their case but that's been no use, because everyone believed up till recently that fingerprints cannot lie. Now we know that they can. So my association is making enquiries of every man who has been convicted mainly on fingerprint evidence and who disputes his guilt. Now let me make it plain that I am not for a moment suggesting that the police are corrupt except in a very few cases. But there's always the possibility of this happening. But, apart from the police, there may always be an enemy of the man who's been charged or the person who actually committed the crime who has arranged for the accused's fingerprints to be transferred.'

'How many cases have you got on your hands at the moment?'

'I'm not sure about that, but I should think there would be about ten or a dozen.'

'You mean you've got ten or a dozen cases where the man's fingerprints were found at the scene of a crime when he says he wasn't there.'

'Something like that,' said Archibald.

'If you're successful in one you'll have a hell of a lot on your hands, won't you?'

'We can cope,' said Archibald. 'D'you know that I employ six whole time investigators and pay them each six thousand a year?'

'Forgive my asking,' said his fellow member, 'but don't you think your money might be better spent in trying to help the victims of crime? It seems to me that at the present day there are too many people going about trying to make it as comfortable as possible in prison for people who have committed horrible crimes and very little indeed is being done for the unfortunate people who have suffered at the hands of those criminals.'

'Yes,' said Archibald, 'you may have a point there. When I've finished dealing with all these fingerprint cases I might see what can be done for some of the victims.'

'If you have any success, you'll never get to the end of the fingerprint cases.'

'We shall, you know. Incidentally I've a very interesting one on at the moment. I've got one of my very best investigators on it, a woman. She isn't anything to look at but my God if she gets her teeth into a case she doesn't give up easily. Rosemary Clinch is a woman in a thousand.'

CHAPTER SEVEN

The Lost Seven Years

In the few seconds which followed Rosemary's recognition of Graham and her advance upon him with outstretched hand Harriet had a lot of thoughts. It might be interesting to have a competition to see the greatest number of thoughts which anyone can cram into a second or, say, two seconds. There is no doubt that, if it were possible to reduce them into words, they would take up more space on a piece of paper than would seem possible. In Harriet's case, as soon as she saw that Rosemary recognised Graham, her immediate reaction was that it was impossible to consider Graham running away with Rosemary. And then she thought of one or two girls whom she had known in her younger days and who lacked charm, sex appeal and, to all intents and purposes, all those qualities which would be likely to make them attractive to men, but who had nevertheless married highly attractive young bachelors or widowers. She even had time to come back to her first thoughts, which were that she couldn't believe Graham had fallen for Rosemary Clinch from a sexual point of view. But she obviously knew him. And then she wondered whether Graham would admit that he knew her. If he were genuinely suffering from loss of memory he might genuinely claim to have no knowledge of the lady. It was also possible that her entrance might spark off a return of his memory. But by this time Rosemary had reached Graham, shaken him warmly by the hand and was starting to speak to Harriet again.

'I was right, you see,' she said. 'I thought I was. I'm very seldom wrong, as a matter of fact. Of course I must be wrong once or twice. I'd never trust anyone who was always right. Would you, Mr Simpkins?'

Harriet looked carefully at Graham. Now she would soon know if all this loss of memory business was a pretence.

'Would I trust anyone who was always right?' said Graham. Harriet at once felt sure that his loss of memory *was* a pretence. He was now playing for time.

'Well,' he went on, 'I suppose it depends who it was. Like most small boys I believed everything my father told me was right. But I didn't stop trusting him when I found out that he wasn't infallible. But might I know to what I owe the pleasure of your coming to see me?'

'Really, Mr Simpkins,' said Rosemary, 'you know perfectly well.'

'You keep on calling him "Mr Simpkins",' said Harriet. 'I've told you our name is Hunt.'

'I'll explain to you later, dear,' said Graham.

'There'll be a great deal to explain,' said Harriet.

Rosemary didn't seem to worry about these interchanges between husband and wife. 'D'you know,' she went on cheerfully, 'I've been in this outfit for three and a half years and I've never had a success yet. Now you're going to be my star case.'

'Case of what?' asked Harriet.

Rosemary appeared to ignore the question. 'It's a great moment for me, I can tell you, Mr Simpkins. I was beginning to believe there'd never be one – for me, that is. The Association has had several triumphs and none of them has been entrusted to me. I don't mind telling you I never expected it. Mr Griffin usually gets the plums but fortunately God took a hand and struck him down. Not seriously, I'm glad to say. But enough to put him out of action. So it all devolves on me.'

'Might I ask where my husband comes into all this?' said Harriet.

'He's the star, of course,' said Rosemary. 'But you can say, if you like, that I'm the producer and the director rolled into one, so I shall get some of the credit. It's about time something like this happened. People are always talking about innocent victims. Girls who are raped, banks which are robbed and old ladies who are mugged and so on. But who are the real innocent victims? They are the raper who didn't, the robber who wasn't there and the mugger who didn't mug. They're the people my association looks after.'

'I gather I didn't rape anyone,' said Graham.

'What a thought, Mr Simpkins,' said Rosemary. 'No, as a matter of fact, half the cases of rape aren't rape at all. The girls simply love it.'

'Miss Clinch,' said Harriet, 'I wonder if you'd mind telling me what all this is about.'

'All in good time, Mrs Simpkins or Mrs Hunt. How would you like me to address you?'

'When I know what it's all about,' said Harriet, 'I'll be able to answer that question better.'

'That's all right, dear,' said Graham. 'Miss Clinch is a little over-excited. I'm sure she'll explain everything in a moment.'

'It's quite simple really,' said Rosemary. 'I can say it in one word. Or is it two? Fingerprints.'

'That's definitely one word,' said Graham.

'That's the answer then. Fingerprints. Mr Simpkins, a great injustice was done. You are completely innocent. The amount of compensation you should get should be prodigious. What's your guess, Mrs Simpkins?'

'I refuse to guess at anything,' said Harriet. 'I want to know what's happened. My husband left me seven years ago and he comes back today with a tale of loss of memory. Where's he been all this time?'

'Surely you know?' said Rosemary.

'As far as I was concerned,' said Harriet, 'he simply disappeared.'

'I suppose he wanted to spare you the shame,' said Rosemary. 'Not only an innocent man but a noble one.'

'Graham,' said Harriet, 'have you been in prison all this time?'

'Yes, darling, I'm afraid I have.'

'He was sentenced to eleven years for a crime which he never committed.'

'It isn't eleven years since he left.'

'Good conduct, darling,' said Graham. 'I came out as soon as I could.'

'Mrs Simpkins,' said Rosemary, 'you're to be congratulated on your husband. A man in a thousand. He spent seven years in prison for a crime he never committed and then apparently walks home as if nothing had happened at all. Now we're going to put all that right. D'you think fifty thousand pounds will be enough? It works out, I believe, at about fifteen to twenty pounds a day.'

'I think you must leave it to me, Miss Clinch,' said Harriet, 'as to whether I'm to be congratulated or not.'

'Well, Miss Clinch,' said Graham, 'if you'd like to write out a cheque for fifty thousand pounds I'll accept it. I'm not greedy.'

'Have a heart, Mr Simpkins,' said Rosemary. 'I don't write the cheque. It's the Government who's going to write the cheque.'

'I thought they weren't very good at writing cheques,' said Graham.

'They're going to be good this time,' said Rosemary. 'What I want you to do is to sign here.' She brought out a form and indicated the place for signature. 'And here. That'll give us authority to go ahead with the case.'

'What crime is Graham supposed to have committed?'

'Don't you even know that?' said Rosemary. 'Stealing one and a half million pounds, as a matter of fact. Quite a tidy sum.'

'A very tidy sum,' said Harriet. 'A hundred pounds a month isn't much out of that.'

'I don't quite understand,' said Rosemary.

'Never mind,' said Harriet. 'That's a matter between my husband and me.'

'The hundred pounds didn't come out of it,' said Graham. 'I never had the one and a half million. Didn't you hear Miss Clinch say that I was innocent?'

'Then why were you convicted?'

'I can answer that one, Mrs Simpkins,' said Rosemary. 'It was a gross miscarriage of justice. The only evidence against him was that his fingerprints were found on the safe where the money was.'

'How did he explain that if he wasn't there?' asked Harriet.

'He couldn't,' said Rosemary.

'If his fingerprints were found on the safe and he couldn't explain why they were there, I don't see where the miscarriage of justice comes in,' said Harriet.

'That's what the jury thought,' said Rosemary.

'I don't blame them,' said Harriet.

'Nor do I,' said Rosemary.

'Then what's all this business about fifty thousand pounds' compensation?' asked Harriet.

'They were his fingerprints all right,' said Rosemary, 'but he never put them there.'

'Then how did they get there?'

'I hoped you'd ask that question.'

'I have asked it.'

'It was discovered a year or so ago,' said Rosemary, 'that you could transfer fingerprints. For example, I put my fingerprints on this table. You can see them on the smooth surface. Well, an expert can take that fingerprint off the table and put it anywhere he likes. It's a skilled job but not all that difficult if you know how. The police admit that it can be done.'

'So you're suggesting that he was framed by the police. Why on earth should the police want to frame somebody of perfectly good character for a crime that had nothing to do with him?'

'The police didn't frame him,' said Rosemary.

'Then who did?'

'The man who instigated the whole thing.'

'Have they caught him then?'

'Unfortunately not at the moment, but the police have obtained evidence from a man who was recently convicted that he actually transferred the fingerprints himself.'

'But how was my husband mixed up with this robbery at all?' asked Harriet.

'I'll explain that to you later, dear,' said Graham.

'And who had the million and a half pounds?' asked Harriet.

'The man goes under various names,' said Rosemary. 'Costello is one of them, but he uses others, I believe.'

'Not Simpkins, by any chance?' said Harriet.

'Certainly not,' said Rosemary.

'Or Hunt?'

'Not as far as I know.'

'Have the police any idea where he is now?'

'They think he's abroad.'

'He'd obviously go abroad,' said Graham. 'A mere million and a half pounds should last him more than seven years.'

'I suppose it would,' said Harriet, 'even if he paid a hundred pounds a month out of it.'

'You keep on mentioning a hundred pounds a month,' said Rosemary. 'I don't understand where this comes in.'

'Never mind, Miss Clinch,' said Graham.

'But I do mind. If there are any loose ends to be tied up I want to tie them up. Let me think. Ah! Suppose that, while Mr Simpkins was in prison, he arranged for somebody to pay you a hundred pounds a month. Is that it?'

'Right as usual, Miss Clinch,' said Graham.

'And where do you say he got the money to pay that from?' asked Harriet.

'I wouldn't know,' said Rosemary, 'would I? I don't know anything about Mr Simpkins' finances.'

'It would be much easier for him if he had part of the million and a half pounds, wouldn't it?' said Harriet. 'Supposing he and Mr Costello were in it together and shared the swag between them? Mr Costello didn't particularly want to be caught, so he left Mr Simpkins' fingerprints on the safe instead of his own. That would account for everything, wouldn't it?'

'Are you suggesting that your husband was a party to this crime?' said Rosemary.

'It looks very like it to me,' said Harriet.

'But that wouldn't suit us at all,' said Rosemary. 'If he was a party to the crime he could have got eleven years for just that. If he only got half the money or even none of it. Tell me that's not true, Mr Simpkins.'

'Of course it isn't,' said Graham. 'Why should I want to steal a million and a half pounds from a bank?'

'I can answer that one,' said Harriet. 'Greed. That's why people steal.'

'But really, darling, you always found me perfectly honest in everything, didn't you? I don't cheat the Inland Revenue and when people have mistakenly sent me a bill for too little I've pointed out the mistake. If the call box telephone suddenly starts pushing money out I always put it back. Why should I suddenly go off the deep end and help to steal a million pounds or more?'

'Yes, Mrs Simpkins,' said Rosemary, 'why should he?'

'People do these things,' said Harriet. 'I quite agree it isn't like my husband to have done it but then it isn't like him to have gone off and left me without telling me anything about it. Or to have come home pretending that he'd lost his memory. Miss Clinch, before you take up anything on my husband's behalf, I think it would be a good idea if I had a word with him privately.'

'By all means,' said Rosemary.

'Then would you very much mind going into the sitting room while we have a chat together?'

Graham intervened. 'Don't you think Miss Clinch might be able to help by filling in a few gaps or something of that sort?' he said.

'When I've found out what the gaps are,' said Harriet, 'Miss Clinch will no doubt be good enough to try to help. In the meantime I want to have a word with you alone.'

'Of course,' said Rosemary. 'Very natural. If I were a married woman that's exactly the course I would have taken myself. I'll tell you one day, if you like, why I'm not a married woman. Personally I think that marriage is the foundation of all happiness. I couldn't bear not being married.'

'I don't quite understand,' began Harriet.

'You're so quick, Mrs Simpkins,' said Rosemary. 'How can I say I'm not married and then say I couldn't bear it if I weren't married? That's what you'd like to know. If you can keep me waiting, I can keep you waiting too, so I'll give you the answer to that when I come back from your sitting room. Perhaps you'd show me the way, please.'

Rosemary got up and Harriet took her to the door which led into the sitting room and opened it.

'Would you care for a cup of coffee and a biscuit while you're waiting?'

'That's most kind. But might I have a glass of milk instead? It will not only take less of your time but I shall enjoy it more. Have you by any chance a digestive biscuit?'

'Fortunately,' said Harriet, 'we have. I won't be long, darling,' said Harriet meaningfully as she and Miss Clinch went out of the room.

As soon as they'd gone, Graham got up and looked at himself in the glass. He smiled a little self-consciously, opened his mouth as though he were going to say something and then shut it again. After looking around a little nervously, he eventually sat down and gave the appearance of being absolutely composed. Suddenly the telephone rang. Graham hesitated for a moment and then answered it.

'Graham Hunt speaking,' he said. 'Yes, I said Graham Hunt. I should sit down if I were you. You must be George. How are you, George, after all this time? I'm so glad you rang. I wanted to thank you so much for looking after Harriet while I was away. It is good of you. Do let me know if it's been any expense to you. I should hate you to be out of pocket. Yes, Harriet's here but she's busy for a moment. You must come and have a drink with us sometime. Fine, thank you. Fine. No, everything's perfectly all right. Where've I been all the time? I'll tell you when we have that drink. Meantime I'm so glad you rang. Have you any message for Harriet? You think perhaps you'd better not come along tonight? Yes, I think you're probably right. My coming home all of a sudden has been a bit of a shock to her, poor girl, but she'll soon get over it and then we'll all three have a drink together. I hope it hasn't been too much of a shock to you, George. Now I'm afraid I can't go on talking any more. Harriet's just coming back. Goodbye, George. Look forward to seeing you.' Graham put down the receiver. As he did so Harriet came in.

'Who was that?' she asked.

'George.'

'What did you tell him?'

'I asked him for a drink.'

'Did he seem upset when he heard you?'

'Well, we haven't got telephone television yet, so I couldn't see the expression on his face, but I must say that I should have liked to.'

'I suppose,' said Harriet, 'it's as good a way of doing it as any.'

'Then you've made up your mind to stay with me,' said Graham.

'I've done nothing of the sort,' said Harriet. 'After we've had our little chat I shall probably go straight round to him and stay with him too, but I'll hear what you have to say first.'

'I wish you'd given Miss Clinch a cup of coffee,' said Graham, 'and then I could have had one too.'

'You're going to have nothing at all until we've had this out.'

'D'you think we'll finish by dinner time, dear?'

'I've no idea,' said Harriet, 'and it won't help you to be facetious.'

'I'm sorry,' said Graham. 'I'm always inclined to be facetious when things are really serious. D'you know when the judge gave me eleven years I actually said: "Why not twelve or ten?" '

'I wondered that,' said Harriet.

'I'm afraid he never told me,' said Graham. 'I said it under my breath, as a matter of fact. If I had said it aloud he might have made it twelve just to oblige. You could write and ask him, I suppose. I'm sorry, dear, I shouldn't have said that. Now, fire away.'

But Harriet couldn't begin immediately. There were so many questions that she wanted to ask that she couldn't at first think where to begin. Eventually she started.

'I simply wouldn't have believed it of you, Graham. I don't know what you've done or what you haven't done, but one thing I know for certain is that you've lied to me like a trooper.'

'That's perfectly true, darling,' said Graham, 'but I really don't know why troopers should get all the blame. I should have thought that politicians and small boys would be better examples. Admittedly trooper is a little easier to say and it has a good sharp sound about it.'

'If you go on like this, Graham,' said Harriet, 'I shan't ask you any more questions. I shall simply pack my bag and go straight to George. The only chance of keeping me as your wife is, first, to satisfy me that everything you now tell me is true and if, I say *if*, I am satisfied with your explanation of how you came to go to prison, I'll think about it.'

'All right,' said Graham, 'I do want you to stay with me. Really I do.'

'First of all then tell me when you were let out of prison.'

'This morning.'

'Why did you come back with that absurd story of having lost your memory?'

'It seemed the easiest way. It would save me explaining so many things. Obviously I was quite wrong because I've got to explain them now.'

'Well you'd better start explaining them. First of all why did you suddenly leave me?'

'I didn't intend to but I couldn't help myself. I was arrested.'

'For the bank robbery?'

'Yes.'

'But I'd have seen your picture in the paper.'

'It never was in the paper. They hoped to get some evidence of identification from a member of the public and, if my picture had been in the paper, my lawyers would have said that was how he'd been able to identify me.'

'That's all very well before the case was over, but, after you were convicted, why wasn't your picture in the paper?'

'I did a deal with the police,' said Graham. 'I gave them some quite useful information and promised them more if they'd see to it that my picture was not published and they kept their word and so did I.'

'I gather you were convicted under the name of Simpkins?'

'That's quite right. I'd established my identity as Simpkins in a place called Risborough.'

'How d'you mean you established your identity?'

'Well, darling, you know that I used to go away from time to time. I told you that it was on the firm's business.

Sometimes it was but sometimes it wasn't. I spent that time establishing myself as Simpkins in Risborough.'

'Was that because there was another woman?'

'There never has been another woman – not even in prison. Sorry.'

'Then what on earth was the object?'

'This may seem a little odd to you.'

'Nothing is going to seem odd to me,' said Harriet, 'after what you've already told me, but I've warned you once and I shan't warn you again that, if you don't tell me the real truth and the whole truth this time, I shall most certainly leave you. I probably will anyway. Now, what was your object in setting up a separate identity as Simpkins in Risborough?'

'It is a little difficult to explain, but I'm a sort of Walter Mitty, I suppose. There's always been a lust for adventure inside me. I expect you've had daydreams. Girls must have them too. I've had them all my life. I mean, as I was on the way to the office, I used to have daydreams of every kind. Always of some adventure and with me as the hero. You say that's absurd in a man of forty-five. All I can say is that it happened. I can't tell you the number of times I've been walking along Lombard Street, visualising a raid on a bank and me capturing the chief villain with a rugger tackle, despite the fact that he was firing a gun. You know how keen I was at watching rugger. That's because I was never any good at it. How often I've visualised myself as playing full back for England. A sort of English J P R Williams. You've no idea. It makes me look like a silly boy. Well, so I am and so I suspect are quite a number of people whom neither of us would have thought it of. I hate telling you this now because it makes me look a pretty good idiot and I daresay you think I'm one anyway. But I'm fighting to keep you, so it's all got to come out.'

'But why did you have to go away to establish a separate identity? You appeared to be happy at home, we had just enough money and we loved each other, we listened to music, we looked at television, we've got quite enough friends and amusing acquaintances. Add your daydreams to all that. Why wasn't that enough?'

'I suppose it should have been, and I must say I felt very odd indeed when I did take a room in Risborough in the name of Simpkins. I nearly came home the next day.'

'Why did you go at all? What were you to do there?'

'To tell you the truth,' said Graham, 'I was playing cops and robbers.'

'What on earth d'you mean?'

'I used to get very angry at the way there were so many bank robberies and that sort of thing and that so few people were caught. I know the police are hopelessly undermanned and that they have a very difficult job, but all the same it used to give me a lot of frustration every time I read about an incident. I wouldn't have done anything about it if I hadn't happened to meet a chap in a pub one day. He was in a drunken confidential mood and whispered to me: "D'you see that chap over there? Well, he's worth a million pounds at least. He's going to be worth a lot more." "What is he?" I asked. "That would be telling," he said. When I'd had a drink or two, although I was absolutely sober, I suddenly had an idea. I left my talkative friend and went to another part of the pub where the man in question couldn't see me. I then went up behind him and tapped him smartly on the shoulder. He spun round as though he had been shot. I knew then that he must be a criminal frightened of arrest. I apologised and said I'd made a mistake and thought he was a friend of mine. I decided to find out a little more about him and by meeting my talkative friend again and plying him with drinks I discovered that my suspect went under the name of "Costello", that he was an educated man and that he was in all probability responsible for several of the big bank robberies that had taken place, but that he didn't actually take part in the raids himself. Finally I discovered that he lived in Risborough in a big house there. At that stage I didn't quite know what I was going to do but eventually I decided that I'd go to Risborough, establish a separate identity for myself under a new name and somehow or other at the golf club or somewhere like that I would get to know Mr Costello.'

'Why didn't you tell me any of this?'

'Because you'd have told me not to be a bloody fool and if you found that I was really going to do it you would have tried to stop me.'

'And I would have saved you seven years in prison if I had.'

'You can see for yourself that, if I'd wanted to play cops and robbers, I should have to do it on my own and see that you knew absolutely nothing about it.'

'You certainly succeeded in doing that. What happened?'

'Eventually I got to know Mr Costello and, quite cleverly as I thought, I made it appear to him that I was a sort of small time crook who could do odd jobs for him quite usefully. In this way I hoped to learn of his plans for some big coup. Then all I had to do was to go to the police, let them know and they'd catch the lot of them. All went well and I learnt of a big coup which was going to take place, a very big one indeed. But unfortunately for me Costello suspected me all the time. He gave me a date for the coup, which was about three weeks after it actually took place. After it had taken place a detective came and interviewed me and asked me if I had any objection to my fingerprints being taken.'

'You had nothing whatever to do with the robbery?'

'Nothing whatever.'

'Then why on earth did they want your fingerprints?'

'You'll see,' said Graham. 'That's what I thought, and as I had an absolutely clear conscience I said I had no objection at all and gave my fingerprints. And, if you please, these were the only fingerprints which were shown to be on the safe. The raid went through perfectly, like all others, and fortunately no one was hurt. But the gang got away with about a million and a half pounds and the only thing the police had to show for it was my fingerprints on the safe. After my first interview with the police I had a feeling that I might be in some sort of a mess so I surrendered my insurance policy, went to a solicitor, gave him the money and told him to send you a hundred pounds a month until it gave out or I gave him further notice. I warned him that in no circumstances was he to disclose who I was. Actually, of course, he didn't know who I was. I went to him under the name of Simpkins.'

'But the bank manager said he still had the policy,' said Harriet.

'I told him not to tell you that I had cashed it, so he had the alternative of breaking my instructions or telling an untruth. You weren't his customer and he didn't know what the relationship was between you and me when I disappeared. In those circumstances he naturally chose to obey my instructions.'

'All right,' said Harriet, 'you surrendered the policy so as to pay me, but once you'd been convicted and were in prison why couldn't you let me know? Didn't you think of my position at all? It was a dreadful thing just to leave me

THE LOST SEVEN YEARS

lke that. I was pretty sure you must have gone off with

like that. I was pretty sure you must have gone off with another woman. I'm not so sure that you didn't anyway.'

'Would you have preferred to know that I was in prison instead of going off with another woman?'

'Certainly.'

'Or killed in an accident?'

'I'm not sure.'

'You bloodthirsty little thing,' said Graham. 'But how would you have felt if a police officer had suddenly come to your doorstep and told you that I was doing eleven years? It sounds like a lifetime. Even seven years at the beginning seems like that.'

'It must have been awful,' said Harriet, 'but I'd certainly have preferred to know. At least you'd have been alive.'

'And not with another woman,' said Graham. 'But think of your friends and neighbours. They'd have been so terribly sorry for you. Could you have borne it? What have you done to deserve a husband who was in prison? And think of those dreadful visits to the prison itself. And the letters I'd have written from prison. Wouldn't you prefer to think of me as dead than rotting away in one of those grim places?'

'I must say,' said Harriet, 'they don't seem to have done you much harm. You haven't been out a day yet and you're as chirpy as a sparrow. Just like you always were.'

'I've been in an open prison for a year,' said Graham. 'That's quite a help.'

'But when it came nearer the time for your release, why couldn't you have let me know?'

'Actually I thought about that but it would have meant your knowing and eventually all our friends and relations knowing that I'd been in prison. So I thought of the lost memory stunt. I admit it's a corny one and that there are very few which are genuine. But there are a few, and I was stupid enough to think I could get away with it. I wanted to start a new life where I'd left off. I'd no idea that Miss Clinch would be pursuing me. I didn't tell her my real name when she came to see me in prison. How did she get hold of me? Did she tell you?'

'She didn't.'

'You see,' said Graham, 'I was very careful when I was leading my double life. As Simpkins I never carried anything which could connect me with you or with Graham Hunt. When I came out of prison they gave me back all the things I had when I went in. That's why they were all dated 1969. There's nothing on them which identifies who I am. So just as I successfully led the life of Mr Simpkins in Risborough I thought I could come back to you and lead the life of Mr Hunt.'

'But why didn't you have the sense to realise that I might have found somebody else? You must have known that I'd be lonely. I'm not a hermit by nature. And can't you see how unfair it was to me suddenly to turn up as though nothing had happened?'

'It was selfish, I agree,' said Graham, 'but when I came back, I didn't want to be known as a man with a conviction for a bank robbery and a sentence of eleven years against me. And I must say I didn't see why I shouldn't get away with it. This damned society of Miss Clinch's – what's it called? The Citizens' something or other.'

'The Citizens' Protection Association.'

'They're just busybodies. I don't want their beastly protection.'

'But you wouldn't mind their fifty thousand pounds?'

'Indeed I would not. But, as you heard, they're not going to give it to me. They're just going to make a fine thing for themselves out of my case. An innocent man convicted on fingerprint evidence! A huge success for them and all it will do for me is to give me more and more publicity and lots of people will say that I must have been doing it all the time and that's why they arrested me. And if I was innocent that time what about the times when I was never caught?'

'Graham,' said Harriet, 'you're not going to evade answering awkward questions just by talking a lot. What I want to know first is how am I to know that you're telling me the truth now? You lied to me for a solid half hour and, if it is the truth that you're telling me now, you only tell it because you're forced to by Miss Clinch.'

'We mustn't forget her,' said Graham. 'She must have finished her glass of milk by now and perhaps the digestive biscuit as well. But why should you think that I should still be lying to you?'

'For one thing people very rarely get eleven years or seven years or whatever you did get for nothing and I have a feeling that you were mixed up in this robbery in one way or another. How did the police get on to you at all?'

'Because Costello or one of the gang must have given them my fingerprints. I'd been associating with him and had had drinks at his house. It was easy enough for him to take fingerprints off a glass and then transfer them to the safe and later on as an informer to send them to the police and give them my name and address. Naturally the police came and looked me up, found the fingerprints were a true bill and that was the end of that.'

Harriet said nothing.

'You still don't believe me then?'

'If I don't, it's your own fault.'

'But what have I got to gain by lying now?'

'I don't know,' said Harriet, 'but there's so much I now know that I didn't know about you that nothing really would surprise me.'

'Aren't you just a little pleased that I've come back?'

'I don't know what to say.'

'Would you have liked the lost memory story to be the true one?'

'I almost think I would.'

'But that would have meant living with a man who was liable to go insane at any moment. You said that yourself.'

'But you were prepared to let me do that,' said Harriet. 'If your pretence had come off, you'd have been perfectly happy to leave me sitting on a volcano which might become active at any moment. That was a dreadful thing to do.'

'I suppose it was,' said Graham, 'but you mustn't blame me too much for doing the wrong thing. I've been in prison for seven years. It's pretty awful to be there anyway, but to be there when you know you're innocent is something no one can appreciate unless he has experienced it. Whatever you think of me, can I stay? Are you prepared to give up George? You couldn't really have enjoyed living with him for long. He's such an ass.'

'He's been extremely kind to me and you've been extremely unkind. He may not have as brilliant a mind as you have but he considers other people's feelings a good deal more than you do.'

'I deserved that, I agree,' said Graham. 'But I did consider your feelings. It's simply that I went the wrong way about it. I attached too much importance to your not knowing about the prison side of it.'

'Was it very awful there?'

'Pretty bad. Missing you was the worst, I think.'

'You have to say that now.'

'Don't forget that you had George. I didn't much fancy any of my cell mates in that way. I did have a bit of luck for a time. I shared a cell with a very cheerful Cockney pickpocket. We whiled away the time by his teaching me some of the tricks of the trade. I believe I could make my living at it if I chose. He reckoned that if you went the right way about it you could get away with it twelve times out of thirteen.'

'I take it you won't be trying that,' said Harriet. 'What d'you want to do now? Go back to the office?'

'Not a bit of it,' said Graham. 'What I'd really like to do is to put my feet up. I've had the seven lean years and now I want the seven fat ones.'

'Who's going to provide for them?' said Harriet.

'That's a point. Hadn't we better have Miss Clinch back and see what she can do about it? Fifty thousand pounds would go some way towards starting me on a new life.'

'I'll go and fetch her,' said Harriet. 'If George rings again while I'm out of the room, I want to speak to him myself.'

'You shall,' said Graham.

Harriet went out and she'd only been gone a few seconds when the telephone rang.

'Poor old George,' said Graham, and lifted the receiver. 'This is Graham Hunt speaking. What's that? No one of that name lives here. No, I'm quite sure. My wife and I have lived here for twenty years. We bought the house from a man called Wellerby. I don't know how the mistake occurred. I'm sorry. You'd better ask Directory Enquiries. Goodbye.' He replaced the receiver. A few minutes later Harriet came back into the room with Miss Clinch.

'Who was that? George?'

'No. Just a wrong number,' said Graham. 'Miss Clinch, before we go into anything else, would you mind telling me how you knew I was here?'

'Quite simple. The police told me. They've been very cooperative with our Association. Ever since they discovered that fingerprints could be transferred we've kept in touch with them because we've been going into all the cases where a man's fingerprints were at the scene of a crime and he denied having committed it. That's how we came across yours.'

'Yes,' said Graham, 'but how did the police know that I'd come here?'

'They put what is called, I believe, a tail on you.'

'Did they, confound them. Now I come to think of it, I did have a feeling that I was being followed. I don't quite know why. I saw no one.'

'As soon as they telephoned me,' said Miss Clinch, 'I was on my way and here I am. No time wasted, you see.'

'Another thing, Miss Clinch, that you might be able to help about. Have you interviewed many prisoners in prison?'

'Quite a number.'

'Perhaps you'd explain to my wife what it's like going to prison.'

'It's perfectly horrible. I don't recommend it.'

'What are the interviews like, between husband and wife and so on?'

'They vary a lot. In some cases they're not too bad because they take place in a room where they can have coffee or tea or something. They sit at separate tables. But at other places they have a wire mesh between them and there's a prison officer there all the time.'

'If you were married, Miss Clinch,' began Graham but Rosemary interrupted.

'That reminds me. I was going to tell you about that. My husband's a very religious man but he doesn't believe in civil marriages.'

'Why not, may I ask?' said Harriet.

'Marriages are made in Heaven and not by registrars. And marriages are forever. There can be no question of divorce. So what we did was to get married in church.'

'Then you are married,' said Graham.

'Only in the sight of God,' said Rosemary. 'After the vicar had pronounced us man and wife we told all our friends to go home and we refused to sign the register.'

'Forgive my mentioning it, Miss Clinch,' said Graham, 'but does that mean that you're both single in the eyes of the law? You're both earning your own living so you don't have to pay as much income tax as if you were married in the eyes of the law.'

'That is what you may call a spin-off,' said Rosemary, 'but it had nothing whatever to do with our decision.'

'Well, Miss Clinch, which would you have preferred? For your husband to have disappeared altogether or to have been sent to prison for eleven years for a serious crime?'

'I can't conceive any of those things happening,' said Rosemary.

'Suppose he had been sent to prison,' said Graham. 'How would you have found life knowing that he was in one of those awful places and only being able to visit him, say, once a month?'

'Fortunately,' said Rosemary, 'I married a man who could in no circumstances have been sent to prison.'

'Not even if his fingerprints had been wrongfully placed by somebody at the scene of a crime?'

'Nobody would want to do that to my husband.'

'Why should they want to do it to me?'

'You must know better than I do, Mr Simpkins. My husband has never associated knowingly with a member of the criminal classes. You did associate with Mr Costello.

Anyone who does a thing like that is taking a chance, isn't he?'

'I wanted to have him caught red-handed.'

'But instead you were,' said Rosemary. 'Now we'd better get on with the business in hand. We are proposing to ask the Home Secretary on your behalf to refer the matter to the Court of Appeal on the ground that fresh evidence has been discovered since your trial. In my opinion the Home Secretary will be bound to refer the matter to the court. When you were convicted it was not known that fingerprints could be transferred and the result was that, as your fingerprints were found on the safe and you couldn't explain how they came to be there, you were bound to be convicted. And now we have strong evidence that your fingerprints were transferred. Someone tipped off the police with an anonymous telephone call that you were the man they were looking for. All you could say was that you weren't there, but you couldn't give any explanation of your fingerprints being found there. The same will one day happen with television photographs. Television cameras secretly placed in a strongroom, for example, will photograph people who come in there. They will say that they never came there but photographs will prove that they did. And then one day it will be shown that photographs can be substituted and so it will go on. It will be our Association's business to look into these things. I must say that nobody seems to be very grateful to us. And you, Mr Simpkins, haven't said thank you to me yet. Admittedly I haven't had any results so far, but you could at least have thanked me for trying.'

'Oh,' said Graham, 'I do very much indeed, Miss Clinch. It was extremely kind of you and your Association.'

'That's easy enough to say now, Mr Simpkins. Now that I've asked you to. But you can't say that your thanks were given exactly spontaneously.'

'Miss Clinch,' said Graham, 'if you'd just been released from prison after serving seven years for a crime which you hadn't committed you mightn't say exactly the right thing within a few hours of being released.'

'A good point, Mr Simpkins,' said Rosemary. 'I think perhaps I owe you an apology. You know it's difficult when you see a man in ordinary civilian clothes in his own house talking as though he hadn't a care in the world to visualise him in prison clothes in a cell in prison. No, I'm very sorry. You apologised to me but the boot is on the other foot. Society has done you a great wrong and we can't apologise to you too much for it. Even if you get fifty thousand pounds or more, nothing can compensate you for those two thousand five hundred days and nights spent in prison. To be deprived of one's liberty is a terrible thing in any event, but to be deprived of it in one of our prisons is quite appalling. You spend most of your time locked up in a cell, if you're lucky by yourself and if you're unlucky with two wholly incompatible people. In many prisons there are still the most rudimentary sanitary arrangements. There's very little exercise and very little work. And when people use the expression "rotting away in prison" it doesn't seem to me at all too strong a phrase to use. In what is supposed to be an enlightened twentieth century it's an absolute disgrace that human beings should have to live as they have to do in prison, whatever they've done. Admittedly prison is meant to be a punishment but in my view the deprivation of liberty is quite sufficient punishment if served in tolerable conditions. I am talking now of people who deserve to be in prison, people who have committed crimes against society which cannot be overlooked. But when you think of innocent people who are in prison, it's too appalling to think of their situation. It's surprising to me that you didn't go mad. The thought of an innocent man contending against the humiliation, the degradation and the physical unpleasantness of prison in addition to being deprived of his liberty for years fills me with horror and, if lying down in the middle of Whitehall would help to get you your compensation, I should be very much inclined to lie down.'

'Fortunately,' said Graham, 'I don't think that your lying down in Whitehall would do anything except give a busy police force a little unnecessary extra work to do.'

'I think you're right, Mr Simpkins, so I won't try it.'

'If your Association spent its time and its money in trying to help the victims of crime,' put in Harriet, 'I'd have some sympathy with it. Prison wasn't meant to be a rest cure.'

'That's what most people say,' said Rosemary, 'and that's one of the reasons why my Association exists. I quite agree that more should be done for the victims of crime but that doesn't mean to say that we should act like barbarians towards those who have been convicted. Well, Mr Simpkins, as you've been good enough to sign the forms, I don't think there's anything else I need worry you with at the moment. The police will want to see you, I expect, but I take it that you won't have any objection to that. Who would you like to represent you? The solicitor who represented you at the trial would probably do it if you wanted him to. I imagine you'd like to have him again. One of your counsel is now a judge and the other has given up the Bar, so we will have to employ somebody else.'

'Why do I want all these lawyers?' said Graham.

'You'll appeal, of course,' said Rosemary. 'I take it you don't want to argue points of law at the Court of Appeal yourself.'

'What are the points of law?' asked Graham. 'I gather from you that the simple point is this. I was convicted on the evidence of fingerprints. It is now accepted that fingerprints can be transferred and there is some evidence that my fingerprints were transferred. I say I wasn't there and I may add I wasn't.'

'My dear Mr Simpkins,' said Rosemary, 'if you want to represent yourself in a court of law there's nothing to stop you, but however intelligent you may be, if you'll take my advice you'll leave legal matters to the lawyers. You've got a conviction against you and you want it set aside. That can only be done in a court of law. If you're worried about the expenses, you needn't be because, in the first place, if the Home Secretary refers the matter to the Court of Appeal you would certainly get legal aid. Of course, if you've got a lot of money tucked away somewhere, the legal aid people will be able to get it from you later. If you haven't any, it won't cost you anything at all. Apart from all that, if you didn't get legal aid I strongly suspect that my Association would be prepared to foot the bill.'

'I see your point,' said Graham. 'I must admit I should feel very lost trying to argue a case in a court of appeal, so thank you very much. I will accept legal aid if you can get it for me. What's the next step?'

'The next step,' said Rosemary, 'is for my Association to forward these documents to the Home Secretary and, as soon as we've had a decision from him, I will let you know. You're not thinking of going abroad, I hope?'

'It's always possible,' said Graham, 'but I haven't had much time to think what I'm going to do.'

'If you do decide to go abroad, please let me know in advance.'

'I'll certainly do that and I'm most grateful to you for all the trouble you and your Association are taking.'

A few moments later Rosemary left.

'Blast that woman,' said Graham, as soon as she'd gone. 'Now I shall have the police and the lawyers and, oh Lord, there'll be the Press too. They'll want to photograph us. I'm surprised they're not here already. We'd better be pleasant to them and then they'll be nice to us.'

'What about the television people?' said Harriet.

'Them too. You won't tell them my lost memory story, will you.'

'Of course not.'

'They'll ask you how you felt when I was in prison. They always ask that. How did you feel when you heard your husband was killed in an accident? And they'll ask you if you visited me in prison. You'd better say that we decided it was so awful when you went away. That must be true enough. And counting the days till the next visit. I'd have had to count about two thousand five hundred days. And the number of times I've watched the date getting nearer and nearer – the date on my cell door. One of the most sensible things the authorities do as soon as a man goes into prison is to put on his cell door the anticipated date of release. If he misbehaves himself it must be awful if one loses enough marks to have the date postponed.'

'Don't start to feel sorry for yourself, Graham,' said Harriet. 'Up to now you've been very good. If you start allowing things like that to prey on your mind it may be bad for us both.'

Graham put his arm round her. 'Thank you for the "us both",' he said. 'Will you tell the Press anything about George?'

'No, why should I?'

'One of them may well ask how you've managed during the seven years and whether you've had any boyfriends.'

'What the hell has that got to do with them?'

'It's got everything to do with them,' said Graham. 'People blame the Press but it's the public that's at fault. When journalists ask these horrible questions of people who've just been involved in accidents or whose near relatives have been involved in accidents – things like what did you feel when you saw your baby cut to pieces – nothing quite as bad as that but almost as bad – it isn't the journalists' fault. It's because unfortunately too many of us, whether we admit it or not, love reading these horrible little intimate details. If we didn't, the Press wouldn't report them. They only give the public what they want or what they think they want. Usually they're right. Don't most of your friends who take a paper read the gossip columns in it? Even a so-called respectable paper has got gossip columns. I don't mind admitting that I read them too. Men are just as bad as women in that respect. It's human nature. Everybody loves a little bit of dirt and, if they didn't, the Press wouldn't give it to them. There's no need to tell the truth to the Press. The public have got no right whatever to know that you and George were having it off while I was in jail.'

'Don't use that horrible expression about me, please,' said Harriet, 'and anyway it isn't true.'

'I'm sorry. All that you've got to say is that you've had no boyfriend and that you were waiting patiently for my release all the time. Oh, I forgot. You've divorced me. You'll have to explain that. Why did you divorce me?'

'Because I couldn't go on waiting for ever, I suppose.'

'Yes,' said Graham, 'but, unless you admit that you didn't know where I was, it wasn't for ever. And in fact you only divorced me at just about the time I'd be coming out of prison. You know, we've got to be a bit careful about this. And then you'll have to explain why we want the decree rescinded. Of course the Press will love that because it will bring some romanticism into it. But we needn't say anything about that for the moment. What I suggest you do when they ask questions is simply to say that you don't think your private life is of any interest to the public and that therefore, without intending any offence to the ladies and gentlemen who are asking you questions, you don't propose to discuss it. And later on when they come and see us and ask why we had the decree rescinded, we simply say that we had it rescinded because that was what we wanted and that we are going to live happily ever after.'

'What are you going to say about your change of name?'

'That's a point. We'd better tell them the truth, pretty well. I shall say that I wanted to try a little detective work on my own account and changed my name for that purpose. Then they'll ask me, I suppose, if you knew anything about it. I shall say you didn't and you can confirm that.'

'They may ask me how I supported myself when you were away,' said Harriet.

'Well,' said Graham, 'I shall tell them about the hundred pounds a month. Incidentally I think I'd better get on to the bank manager and let him know that I've returned. Is he the same man, by the way? What's his name? Gardiner?'

'That's right. He's still there.'

'All right. I'll get on to him.' Graham went to the telephone and dialled a number. 'Gardiner's a nice old boy,' he said. 'I expect he was very helpful when you went to him.'

'He did what he could,' said Harriet, 'but it wasn't very much.'

'Ah, here he is. Hullo? Yes. May I speak to the manager, please? Say I'm speaking for Mrs Hunt of The Cottage, London Lane, near Redgrave. Right. I'll hold on. I thought I'd give him the shock at first hand, rather than let it percolate to him through some clerk or other. Hullo? Hullo? Is that Mr Gardiner? Now you're going to get a surprise, Mr Gardiner. This is Graham Hunt speaking. Yes. Graham Hunt. No, I'm not astonished that you're surprised. I'm very well, thank you. You may well ask. I'd like to come round and see you and have a chat about it. Would tomorrow morning at eleven be convenient? Good. I'll do that. I'm afraid you may read something in the Press about my return but with luck I'll be able to tell you first.'

'Don't let him go,' said Harriet. 'I want to have a word with him.'

'Can't it wait?'

'No. I want to speak to him now.'

'Very well,' said Graham. 'My wife wants a word with you, Mr Gardiner. Here she is.'

Harriet went to the telephone. 'Oh, Mr Gardiner, my husband had a life insurance policy with you for some fifteen thousand pounds. Can you tell me exactly when it was surrendered? I beg your pardon. Are you sure? Would you mind sending for it? Yes, I'll hold on.'

'What on earth's he saying?' said Graham.

'I'll tell you in a moment,' said Harriet.

'It's quite impossible,' said Graham.

'Hullo? Hullo? Yes, Mr Gardiner. Yes. Are you quite sure that this is the only policy and that it hasn't been surrendered? Thank you very much. Goodbye.' Harriet put down the receiver and looked at Graham. Neither of them said anything, for a moment or two. 'So you've been telling me the truth, Graham, have you? About the hundred pounds a month. It came out of the insurance policy, did it?'

At that moment there was a ring at the bell. 'If that's Miss Clinch again,' said Harriet, 'you'd better tell her to stop that appeal.'

'I can explain,' said Graham.

'You've got some explaining to do,' said Harriet. 'I'll go to the door first.'

'No, don't,' said Graham. 'I want to see who it is. Wait a moment.' He went into the next room and then came back five or ten seconds later. 'There doesn't seem to be anybody there.' He went to the door and opened it, looked each way down the road and came back. 'There's not a soul in sight,' he said.

'Never mind about the souls in sight,' said Harriet. 'I want to know the whole truth if you're capable of telling it. You were mixed up with the robbery. My hundred pounds a month came out of it. That's the truth, isn't it?'

'Put like that,' said Graham, 'it certainly isn't. But before I start giving you any explanations I shall have to make a phone call. I ought to have thought of it before. Darling, I'm afraid we may have another visitor.'

Graham went to the telephone and dialled 999. As soon as it was answered he said he wanted the police.

'My number is Redgrave 4276. My name is Simpkins and my address is The Cottage, London Lane, near Redgrave. I'm expecting a visit from a very dangerous armed man. Detective Superintendent Ackroyd of the CID will be most interested in him. His name is Costello. No, not the superintendent's. I told you that's Ackroyd. Thank you.'

He put down the receiver. 'Now let's have a drink.'

'Have we time?' asked Harriet.

'We needn't open the door until we've had one.'

'But you sounded so urgent.'

'If you want someone to hurry, you have to sound urgent. I think a large whisky will do nicely. It's possible he may not come at all but I expect he will.'

Harriet got up and poured out a large whisky for each of them. 'Now, Graham, how much of the truth are you going to tell me this time?'

'More than last time.'

'It had better be.'

'First of all, your hundred pounds a month came from the Midland Bank.'

'I knew that because it was on the cheques.'

'No, I mean from the Midland Bank that Costello's men robbed.'

'And you had nothing to do with it except for the fingerprints?'

'No, I really didn't have anything to do with it. The only thing is – I got all the money.'

'So you did steal it.'

'Oh dear me no. What I told Miss Clinch was perfectly true. I was hoping that the gang would be caught as a result of information I was going to give the police. But what happened was this. As I said, the raid took place several weeks before I thought it was going to. They took away the money in suitcases but the police got to know about this and they had to get rid of them for the moment very quickly. So they dumped them on me. They'd already put my fingerprints on the safe as a precaution but of course I didn't know this at the time. The man who gave me the suitcases told me to put them in safe deposits at once. I would have done that anyway for my own protection, because I shouldn't have liked to have been raided by the police and for them to have found all that money in my possession. So I went off in my car at once, waited until the safe deposits opened and then I put it in three different safe deposits. It was all under the name of Graham Hunt of this address.'

'So that's where my hundred pounds a month came from.'

'Quite right. I was arrested within a few days. So I just had time to take out twelve thousand pounds and take it to the solicitors.'

'Why did you tell me it was from the insurance policy?'

'Well, darling, gently does it. You had a bit of a shock when I walked in. If I had told you ten minutes later that I was worth a million and a half pounds it would pretty well have bowled you over, wouldn't it.'

'You're not worth a million and a half pounds. That money isn't yours.'

'It wasn't Costello's either, was it? His man handed it to me and I got eleven years' imprisonment into the bargain. So I've paid the price. They can't send me to prison again, so why shouldn't I hang on to it?'

'Because it isn't yours,' said Harriet. 'Anyway Mr Costello will tell you why you shouldn't hang on to it, if he comes here.'

'You're right there,' said Graham. 'I ought to have asked to be released from some other prison.'

'Is there anything else you ought to tell me or do I know it all by now?'

'I think you know all that's happened so far,' said Graham. 'But if there are any more questions you'd like to ask, fire away.'

'Presumably,' said Harriet, 'Mr Costello's been waiting seven years to get this money, so I don't suppose he'll want to be kept waiting much longer.'

'I think you're right there. If I know anything about him, he'll have an aeroplane standing by ready to take the money, as soon as he's got it off me, to some little place of his in Europe.'

'What are you going to do about it?'

'What can I do besides what I've done? I've called for the police. Let's hope to God that they come before he does.'

'Suppose they do? Will you tell them where the money is?'

'D'you think I should?'

'Of course. It still belongs to the Bank.'

'I thought we might have gone abroad and lived a new life on my ill-gotten gains. As I've said, I've served seven years for it.'

'You keep on saying that,' said Harriet. 'It doesn't make the slightest difference. You must know that. Prison seems to have made you into a criminal.'

'It's possible,' said Graham. 'It's supposed to have some reformative value. That's if there's anything to reform. But until I went to prison I was a completely innocent person. I still am, as a matter of fact.'

'What about the hundred pounds a month?'

'Oh that,' said Graham. 'They can't send me to jail again because of that. It's a very small part of the million and a half.'

'But you certainly won't be innocent as soon as you keep any part of that money for yourself.'

'Don't you think the state owes me anything?'

'I'm not at all sure that it does,' said Harriet. 'After all, at your trial you could have said where the money was but you kept very quiet about that.'

'If I'd told them where the money was, I might just as well have been sentenced to death.'

'What on earth d'you mean?'

'People like Costello wouldn't stand for it.'

'But you'd be quite safe in prison.'

'You don't know what you're saying,' said Graham. 'It's the one place where you're not safe at all. First of all, they know exactly where you are. Or, if your prison is changed, they can soon find out. And, unless you choose to ask for solitary confinement for the whole of your sentence, you haven't a hope of avoiding having your throat slit or your head bashed in. There are plenty of long-termers who are prepared to murder their fellow prisoners for a sufficient consideration.'

'But what would he get out of it?'

'Costello, you mean.'

'Yes.'

'Quite simply what he'd get out of it would be the example. He'd have shown the underworld what happened to anybody who did him down, either by running off with the money himself or by handing it over to the authorities. That's a thing he wouldn't stand for. So even if I'd felt inclined to do it, I couldn't, out of pure self-preservation.'

'Well, if you keep the money yourself that won't please Costello and his friends any more.'

'I agree,' said Graham, 'but with a million and a half pounds to play with I've a reasonable chance of keeping out of his clutches. If I just handed over the money now, the police couldn't give me permanent protection for twenty-four hours a day, if they'd be prepared to give me any protection at all. We wouldn't have the money to get out of his way ourselves, so I'd simply be a sitting duck. As in fact I am. No, the only way I might be able to be safe is if I hand over the money to Costello when he comes along and take the chance that he doesn't dispose of me as soon as he's laid his hands on the money. And that's a pretty poor chance, as he wouldn't want to have my evidence against him. Believe me I've thought of all the various possibilities but I've also realised – a bit late in the day – that my original idea was unlikely to succeed.'

At that moment there was a ring at the front door bell.

CHAPTER EIGHT

Costello

'I'm afraid this is it,' said Graham.

'What are you going to do?' said Harriet.

'I've no idea. Play it by ear, I suppose. Though what that means in this case, heaven alone knows.' He went to the door and opened it. It was Costello.

'My dear,' he said, 'this is Mr Costello. How nice to see you again.'

Costello came into the room and shut the door behind him.

'You're really pleased to see me, are you?' he said with a polite smile. He was a good-looking man, of about forty-five, with a cultured voice.

'I'm overjoyed,' said Graham.

'Isn't that putting it a bit high?'

'Perhaps a little bit, but I'm really delighted.'

'I take it this is Mrs Simpkins,' said Costello. 'Mrs Simpkins, would you say your husband was a truthful person?'

'Don't bother to answer that,' said Graham. 'She's heard more lies in the last hour than she's probably heard in the rest of her life.'

'Would you say that your last statement to me was one of them?' asked Costello.

'You mean that I was delighted to see you?'

'Precisely.'

'Well, I haven't seen you for a long time.'

'You may have unusual taste,' said Costello, 'but are you usually delighted to see dangerous armed men?'

'How many?'

'One will do to begin with.'

'Can I get you a drink?'

'Yes, please, but I shall want to see the bottle and the glass.'

'What should be in the bottle?' asked Graham.

'Scotch.'

'And in the glass?'

'Nothing until you put in the Scotch.'

'Would you like anything with it?'

'Just a splash, thank you. And keep the syphon in full view, please. I ought to warn you that I *am* a dangerous armed man. And I don't want you to do anything that your wife might regret.'

Graham poured out a whisky and soda and gave it to Costello. 'May we have one?' he asked.

'Why not? There's no hurry is there?'

'None in the world.'

'If you keep this little pantomime going long enough, the police might arrive, don't you think?'

'Why should they?'

'As a matter of fact,' said Costello, 'there's no reason at all why they should. But up till now I think you hoped they would. You had a call a little while ago from a man who wanted to speak to Mr Bannockburn. I like using the names of battles for proper names. Don't you think it's a good idea? Perhaps you've never thought of it? For quite a time I used Agincourt. They're two of the battles I always remember. Agincourt and Bannockburn. Twelve, thirteen, fourteen, fifteen, if you follow what I mean. Bannockburn 1213. Agincourt 1415.'

'Yes, I had a call for a Mr Bannockburn. I said there was no such person living here.'

'And,' said Costello, 'you very helpfully suggested that the caller should seek the aid of Directory Enquiries.'

'So when I dialled 999,' said Graham, 'it was you at the other end. How did you manage that?'

'Since you went to jail, Mr Simpkins, a lot has happened in world technology. I simply tapped your line.'

Graham looked at the telephone. 'What would I get if I dialled 999 now? One of your engineers?'

'Somehow I don't think you'll try, nor will your wife.'

'I don't think either of us will.'

'Good,' said Costello. 'Now shall we get down to brass tacks?'

'There's nothing I should enjoy more,' said Graham. 'It's odd that when I was a child instead of asking for sweets I used to ask for brass tacks.'

'I suppose that's the way he's been talking to you recently?' Costello asked Harriet.

'Something like it,' she said.

'My dear fellow,' said Graham, 'you don't seem to realise that I've only been out of jail an hour or two. You can't expect a chap to rehabilitate himself in that time. I'm not even used to my new found liberty yet. Being able to go where I like and do what I like and so on.'

'Well,' said Costello, 'I'm afraid you can't go where you like or do what you like or so on.'

'So it seems. Well, what can I do for you? You want the money, I suppose?'

'Quite right,' said Costello. 'I don't suppose you've got it here but I want the names of the safe deposit or deposits where you no doubt put it and the keys and any signed authority which may be necessary to enable us to open the safe. Is it all in safe deposits?'

'All but twelve thousand pounds,' said Graham, 'which I hope you don't mind I helped myself to before I went to prison. It was for a very laudable object. I'm sure you would approve of it. To keep my wife while I was in jail.'

'Very well then. Now I'll tell you what's going to happen,' said Costello. 'You'll write out the necessary authorities and you'll take them and the keys and give them to a man you will see outside this house. Just to make sure you go to the right man you'll ask his name and he'll say "Waterloo". Can I watch you from a window in this house?'

'Quite easily from in there,' said Graham and he pointed to the sitting room door.

'Very well. Your wife will come with me while I watch you. If you do anything except hand the keys and the authorities to this man, if you give a signal to anybody else or do anything suspicious, I shall just shoot her. Is that quite plain?'

'It sounds a bit cold-blooded.'

'Of course it's cold-blooded. Perhaps I ought to explain that this is quite normal procedure today. I don't remember if there were many cases before you went to prison, but nowadays the taking of hostages and kidnapping and hijacking is quite common form, so you needn't feel that this is a new departure.'

'That's very comforting,' said Graham.

As a matter of fact, Graham and his fellow prisoners had heard all about hijacking, kidnapping and the taking of hostages. Nearly all the prisoners were as interested as the free population in the sieges at Spaghetti House and Balcombe Street but, oddly enough, quite a number of hardened criminals who made much of their living, when they were not in prison, by violence, burglary and other forms of villainy, objected strongly to any form of blackmail, whether it included the taking of hostages or not. Graham had been quite surprised to find the low opinion of blackmailers held by men who would not hesitate to bash you on the head if you stood between them and their prey. Indeed, one or two blackmailers who at first were inclined to boast about their exploits, soon found that, if they persisted in this attitude, they would find themselves as loathed by their fellow prisoners as sex offenders who preyed on children. The Spaghetti House and Balcombe Street sieges provoked a number of discussions in prison on the subject and there was no doubt that, if there had been a vote about it, it would have gone against the kidnappers. On some occasions when the matter was being discussed the opinions voiced might well have been those of civil servants employed in the Home Office or even of the police. One violent offender with a good many convictions against him was for once entirely on the side of law and order.

'If these bloody foreigners,' Graham remembered him saying, 'keep on giving in, the thing will never stop. On the other hand, if every kidnapper knew that he would get nothing out of the kidnapping and that killing his victim could only make things worse for him in the end, they'd soon give it up.'

Graham had taken part in this argument. 'But what about children?' he had asked.

'What about them?'

'Well,' he had said, 'I daresay the public wouldn't mind a few adults being bumped off in a good cause. But what would they say about children? Suppose the friends of a man charged with murder kidnapped half a dozen children off the street and threatened to kill them one by one unless the murderer was released, they were paid a large sum of money and given a plane to fly to Cuba or somewhere, would the public back a Government which stood firm and allowed children to be killed, if necessary?'

'I quite agree,' said a professional burglar. 'I'd draw the line at children.'

'But what about the future?' asked another. 'If they gave in because of half a dozen children, next time it could be a dozen or twenty-five or a hundred. I say you mustn't give in to blackmail at all, whatever the consequences.'

'I bet you'd give in if your children or your wife were involved,' said a man who was a specialist in bigamy.

'I expect I would,' said the previous speaker, 'but that's personal. No one can be expected to hand over his wife or children without a struggle. But the Government's got to ignore such things. Once it was known that it was no use kidnapping anyone, children, women or anyone else, people wouldn't try.'

'There's one thing you haven't thought of,' said a man who was only in prison for murdering his wife and could not therefore be considered an ordinary criminal. 'Suppose a man got hold of a nuclear bomb and flew over London with it, the Government would have to give him all he asked for.'

Graham had time to remember some of these things before Costello spoke again.

'The man you give the keys and authorities to,' he said, 'will then go off and collect the money. When he lets me know that everything is in order we will tie you both up securely but otherwise leave you, I hope, in the same good condition as you are now both in. But I warn you that, if he doesn't get the money or if you make any false moves of any kind, I shall shoot you both.'

'It's nice of you to be so frank,' said Graham.

'I wouldn't want there to be any misunderstanding,' said Costello.

'Nor would I. It's not a very nice way to spend my first day out of prison.'

'It'll be even more unpleasant,' said Costello, 'if you don't do exactly as you're told. Now you'd better start writing out those authorities. In the meantime your wife can give me another drink.'

Harriet got up and went towards the drinks cupboard.

'And I want to see the bottle and the glass, please. Just whisky and a splash. Thank you. Now, is any special form of authority necessary? Is there any special paper it's got to be written on?'

'No. It can be done on my own writing paper and I've got some here. One of the deposits is in Manchester, another is in Chester and the third's in Bootle.'

'Bootle?' said Costello. 'That's a hell of a way away. It'll take hours to get there. Let me think. Give me a piece of paper to write on.'

Graham gave Costello a piece of writing paper and then Costello sat down, thought for a moment and wrote. When he'd finished, he folded up the piece of paper and gave it to Graham.

'When you give the man the keys and authorities, give him this as well. This means that I shall have to be your guest for quite a little longer than I had expected. I'll have your telephone reinstated and I'm giving instructions for this man to telephone me as soon as he's got all the money. What's your number?'

'Redgrave 4276.'

'Redgrave 4276,' Costello immediately repeated and wrote it down. 'How are you getting on with those authorities?'

'I've done one,' said Graham. 'And you'll want an extra one to get the keys. I haven't got them here. They're at a branch of the Midland Bank, in a small packet. I'll write out an authority for him to collect it.'

'Is it a London branch?'

'No. Liverpool.'

'Bootle and Liverpool? They won't be able to get to them both in time. I'll be here all night. That means, I'm afraid, that I shall have to tie you up during the night and pretty carefully too. I shall want some sleep. You've got some food, I take it.'

'Enough for the three of us,' said Harriet.

'Good. How are those authorities going?'

'I've done the three for the safe deposits,' said Graham. 'Now you want the one for the Liverpool bank.'

'Let's look at the ones you've done,' said Costello. Graham handed them to him. 'I believe some banks have a code they give their customers in case this sort of thing might happen. By putting some sort of word or mark or something, the safe deposit people are alerted to hold the bearer. I just want to warn you that, if anything of that sort happens, I shall kill you both. I shall know if there's been any hitch or whether he's got the money safe and sound, so if you've done anything of that sort you'd better scrap it here and now and start again.'

'I didn't know about these codes,' said Graham. 'But what a good idea. To put a full stop instead of a comma. Instead of getting the money, you get a pass into the police station.'

'Are there any full stops instead of commas?' asked Costello.

'There aren't any full stops or commas.'

'You know what I mean,' said Costello. 'Is there any code of any kind used in those authorities?'

125

'None at all. You can take my word for it.'

'Would you advise me to take his word, Mrs Simpkins?'

'I think you can in this case. You see neither of us wants to be shot.'

'We don't want to be tied up either,' said Graham.

'That, I'm afraid, will be necessary. There might be other things necessary, but that depends upon you. Just a moment.' He unfolded the note which he'd written to give to the man and wrote some more on it. 'I'm not taking any chances,' he added. 'I've told him to telephone every hour from the time he leaves. If he doesn't, I shall know that something has gone wrong.'

'But hang on a moment,' said Graham. 'He might be killed in an accident.'

'I hope for your sake that he isn't.'

'It really would be too bad if you shot both of us because your man was a bad driver.'

'He's a very good driver.'

'Even good drivers have accidents.'

'We must hope for the best. Now have you got that final authority ready? Let's have a look at it.'

Graham handed it to him.

'No full stops instead of commas?'

'None whatever. No semicolons instead of semiquavers, though why there aren't any quavers I really don't know. I hope you realise, Mr Costello, that however lightly we may take it, we're undergoing a considerable ordeal.'

'Let's hope it doesn't become worse. That rests with you. Now, are you ready to go outside?'

'Yes,' said Graham.

'Now, Mrs Simpkins, please come with me.' Costello took a revolver out of his pocket and pointed the barrel into Harriet's back. 'Now,' he said to Graham, 'don't move until I tell you to. When I say the word "Move", open the door, go outside, find the man, just ask him what I said and see that he replies "Waterloo". If he doesn't, it will be the wrong man. There aren't many men lounging about, at least there shouldn't be. I'll have a look.'

Costello went out of the room with Harriet, leaving the door open. From the sitting room he shouted: 'Can you hear me, Mr Simpkins?'

'Yes,' said Graham. 'Quite clearly.'

'The man in question is on the other side of the road, almost opposite your front door. There's nobody else there so there can't be any mistake. Are you ready to go?'

'Yes,' said Graham.

'Right,' shouted Costello. 'Now, don't forget what will happen if there's any mistake. This gun hardly makes any noise. It's got a silencer. Now move.'

Graham opened the front door and went out. He saw the man on the other side of the road, went up to him and said: 'What is your name, please?'

'Waterloo,' said the man.

Without saying any more, Graham handed him the documents, turned round and came back into the house and shut the door. As soon as he was inside Costello came back into the room with Harriet. He still had the revolver in his hand.

'You seem to be behaving very sensibly,' said Costello.

'I usually behave sensibly,' said Graham, 'but this time it doesn't seem as if I had any choice.'

'You haven't. Now I'd better put your telephone in order.' Costello went to the telephone, lifted the receiver and after a second or two he said: 'It's me. Reconnect. That's all I shall want. OK.' He replaced the receiver. 'Now you can dial 999 if you want to.'

'I don't think I want to at the moment,' said Graham.

'I hope your wife doesn't want to either.'

127

'I hate the very idea,' said Harriet.

'As we're going to see quite a bit of each other during the next few hours,' said Graham, 'would you like me to suggest something to entertain you? Are you a bridge player?'

'I used to be but it's not much fun with three.'

'Can I show you a card trick or two? I'm rather good at them. Sleight of hand and all that.'

'There will be no card tricks or any other kind of tricks.'

'What a shame. I learnt a frightfully good one when I was in prison.'

'I ought to warn you that, if you've any tricks in mind, I shall use this. See what I mean? So don't think you'll be able to distract my attention and suddenly lunge at me with a penknife or throw pepper over me or anything of that sort. Because, if you start anything of that kind, I shall shoot first and wonder if you meant anything afterwards. So both of you be very, very careful.'

'Suppose I went to sneeze,' said Graham, 'and put my hand in my pocket to bring out a handkerchief? You might think I was going to bring out a knife or a revolver or something.'

'That's quite simply dealt with,' said Costello. 'Turn out your pockets on to the table, please. Mrs Simpkins, kindly turn out the contents of your bag on to the table. Everything, mind you. Waistcoat pockets. Everything.'

'Do as he tells you,' said Graham to Harriet.

He emptied his pockets and Harriet emptied her bag. When they'd finished, Costello said: 'Nothing else left? Good. Now, Mrs Simpkins, just stand over there, please, with your hands above your head. Mr Simpkins, come here and put your hands above your head while I make sure that there's nothing else left in your pockets. If either of you should make the slightest move, I shall shoot you both.'

Graham and Harriet did what he told them and he put his hands in each of Graham's pockets, discovering nothing.

'Now. Give me your wife's bag, please.' Graham did so. Costello looked through the bag and found nothing in that. 'Right. I'm going to leave everything on the table. If you want to use a handkerchief, you can go to the table after you've asked me if you can use it.'

'Most considerate,' said Graham.

'I think we might have something to eat in about an hour. What we'll do is that we shall all go into the kitchen and I shall watch Mrs Simpkins do the cooking. Mrs Simpkins, if you make the slightest attempt to put any sleeping tablets or other drugs which you may have about the house into it, I shall shoot you both. And while you're doing the cooking, Mrs Simpkins, I shall tie Mr Simpkins up so that he can't be a nuisance to us.'

'I promise not to be a nuisance,' said Graham. 'I should hate to be tied up. I'm claustrophobic in a way. I should find it very frustrating.'

'And that's how you'll find it,' said Costello. 'There's a million and a half pounds at stake and my liberty. If I were caught, I'd go to prison for so long that it wouldn't make any difference to me if I killed you both. That's why I'm not taking any chances. And both of you had better follow my good example.'

'Might I make a suggestion?' said Graham.

'I can't stop you making one but I'd be very surprised if I agreed to it.'

'Why d'you have to treat us as though we're on the side of the police? We're in this together. I've just done seven years and, if it hadn't been for me, there'd be none of the money left. You might have been doing the seven years yourself.'

'What's that got to do with it?' said Costello.

'Surely you're a reasonable man,' said Graham.

'I'm nothing of the sort.'

'Let me put it like this,' said Graham. 'You want to have a lot of money and to be able to enjoy it in safety.'

'That's exactly what I'm going to do.'

'But don't you see that you'll be much more likely to be able to do that if, instead of tying us up and threatening to shoot us, you let us keep a bit of the money and, in return for that, we promise to tell the police nothing about you.'

'What's the good of your promise? As soon as my back's turned, you would break it. People will promise anything with a revolver between their shoulder blades. I would, I know.'

'But we wouldn't. Really we wouldn't. I've got nothing to thank the police for. I don't suppose you've ever been to jail. 'Well, I have. I've done seven whole years. So far I've got nothing out of it except a hundred pounds a month for my wife and threats by you to truss us up like chickens and to shoot us on the slightest provocation. Now, when your chap gets the money, why not let me have say fifty thousand pounds and, in return for that, I shall say nothing whatever to the police about you or, if you like, I'll lead them up the garden.'

'It's no use,' said Costello. 'In the first place I want all the money myself and I wouldn't give you fifty thousand pence. Secondly, you're as slippery as an eel and you'd get your own back on me if you had half a chance. I'd trust you just as far as I could see you and no further.'

'Couldn't I prove it to you in some way?' asked Graham. 'Suppose I ring up the police now and give them some false information about you?'

'And then,' said Costello, 'as soon as I'd gone, all you had to do is to say that you'd said that because you were being covered by a revolver.'

'But surely I deserve something,' said Graham. 'After all, I've given you authority to get the keys, told you where the money is and kept it for you for seven years. Isn't that worth something?'

'I don't care whether it's worth something or whether it isn't. It's not going to get you anything. You can consider yourself lucky if you get out of this without being shot or suffocated when I tie you up and gag you. I'm all right at tying up but I might overdo the gagging.'

'You seem to get pleasure out of torturing us,' said Harriet.

'Don't put ideas into my head,' said Costello. 'Which reminds me, I might as well start tying you up. When I give you the word, I want you to go outside. You'll see another man there. There are two or three, by the way, but they're all on the Waterloo code. I want you to get a bit of cord from him and the procedure will be the same. I'll take your wife into the next room so that I can see what's happening out of the window. When I say the word "Move" you're to go outside and get the cord and if there's any funny business I shall shoot your wife. Is that plain?'

'All too plain,' said Graham.

'Right.' Costello took Harriet into the next room, again putting the revolver barrel in her back, and left the door open. 'Can you hear me?' he called.

'Yes,' said Graham.

'This chap is in the same position as the other one. Are you ready?'

Graham said he was.

'Right then,' said Costello. 'Move.'

Graham opened the door, went outside and asked the other man what his name was and, having received the reply "Waterloo", said he wanted some cord. Having received it Graham returned to the cottage, came in and shut the door. As soon as the door was shut Costello and Harriet came back into the room.

'Put the cord on the table,' said Costello. 'Now, Mrs Simpkins, I want you to lie down on the floor over there.' Harriet lay down facing him. 'Not like that. Face the other way.' Harriet did what she was told. 'That's better. Now, Simpkins, you sit in this chair and put your hands behind you.' As Graham started to obey the order a car was heard drawing up outside. 'Are you expecting anyone?' asked Costello.

'No one in particular,' said Graham, 'but I suppose the police might pay me a call.'

'I'll go and see,' said Costello. 'Come along,' he said to Harriet. She got up and went with him to the next room. 'Yes, it is the police,' said Costello. 'Now, Simpkins, if you want to see your wife again alive you'll go very, very carefully. Let the policeman in and chat to him as though you've all the time in the world. Don't appear anxious or nervous but get rid of him in the end. I'm going to leave this door ajar so that we can hear every word you say. If you make the slightest false move that will be the end of your wife and of you and the policeman too. Is that plain?'

'I'm not to appear anxious or nervous?' queried Graham. 'Humph. Lucky for me I was in the OUDS.'

'If you breathe a word which suggests that you've seen me since you came out of prison, that will be the end of your wife. Make no mistake about that.'

'Look,' said Graham, 'if I prove I'm on your side by getting rid of him and doing everything you say, how about letting us have twenty thousand pounds.'

'I'll talk about that,' said Costello, 'when you've got rid of him.'

CHAPTER NINE

The Hostage

As soon as the bell rang Harriet went with Costello into the sitting room. She felt the whole scene was really rather unreal. This couldn't be happening to her. She, like most other people in the country, had watched on television the sieges at Spaghetti House and in Balcombe Street and, while these events were going on, she had indeed tried to place herself in the position of one of the unfortunate hostages and wondered what she would have felt or done. But 'doing' didn't really come into it. When a man says to you, 'do this or I'll shoot you' and you know that he probably means it, there is little room for doing. But plenty for thinking. She had been fascinated by the scenes on television. She did not know whether it was worse for the wife in Balcombe Street, who was not well, or for her husband who knew she was not well and, in addition, must have suffered physically and mentally from being tied to a chair. Now this is really happening to me, she said to herself. But it can't be. The great thing about the kidnappings and hijackings is that they happen to other people, not to oneself. It was impossible that so many things should have happened to her on one day.

Graham's return was enough of a traumatic experience. And then the gradual elucidation of the truth. That

Graham was really prepared to steal a million and a half pounds was a bigger shock to her than she had realised at the time. She was a woman who lived her life by standards. She seldom consciously did anything which was below the standard which she'd set for herself. And to the best of her knowledge until now Graham had been exactly the same. This was not so much due to a sense of morality or to a belief in God or to a desire to help other people as to make the business of living as simple as possible. She always remembered what her father had said when, having first told her that it did not pay to tell lies, he went on to answer her question as to why it did not pay with a sentence which she had never forgotten.

'Because no one would ever trust you,' he had said.

From that time her object in life, at first unconsciously and later quite consciously, was to ensure that everyone with whom she came in contact trusted her. And this certainly had paid. But there were excuses for Graham. After all, he had been shut up in prison for seven whole years. She had only been in prison now for a few minutes and it seemed like an eternity. She looked at Costello as he stood there two or three yards away from her fingering the revolver. Why was he such a calculating scoundrel? People who said you can tell a criminal from his face were wrong. There was nothing criminal or cruel in his face. He was just an ordinary, good-looking man who might have been a commuting stockbroker, lawyer or anything else. Yet here he was saying quite dispassionately that, if she or Graham did not do exactly as they were told, he would kill them. And she had little doubt that he would. Not because he disliked them but simply because it was necessary in his view in order to attain his object. Was there no compassion in the man at all? Surely everyone had a heart of some kind. Wouldn't this man stoop to pick up an injured child and comfort him? And if he had a heart, what was the way to it? How could she find that way in only just a few minutes? And then she wondered what it would be like to die. Suddenly not to be. She thought of the famous lines in *Hamlet*, which as a small girl she had learnt by heart without appreciating the meaning. How many soldiers in the war and civilians under air attack had thought of the words: *To be or not to be*? In Hamlet's case there was a choice because he was contemplating suicide. But she did not fear the things which he feared. She was not afraid of dreaming after death or of the perils to be encountered the other side of the grave. She was afraid of dying. Simply that. Graham had come back to her and they could start all over again. And yet within a minute or two they might both be dead. She prayed that she would be killed outright. How good a shot was Costello, she wondered? She had been told that a revolver was a very inaccurate firearm in the hands of anybody but an expert. She hoped he was an expert. But he couldn't really mean it. However little time there was left to them, she must try to develop a relationship which would make it impossible for him to kill either of them. That is what the police, with the guidance of psychiatrists, said they were doing in the Spaghetti House and Balcombe Street sieges. And it appeared that they were successful. Indeed, it looked as though at least one of the hostages in Spaghetti House became a friend of one of his captors. He certainly went to see him after he was in prison. What could she say to this man which would start the right sort of relationship? A relationship which would make it impossible for him to carry out his threat. How should she begin? It would be embarrassing to plead for mercy. If only she had more time she might be able to introduce some subject which interested them both. Croquet or chess, for example. She even smiled slightly when she thought of the old joke, which it would now be illegal to tell: 'Oh we couldn't think of eating you,' said the cannibal to the missionary, 'We're all Christ's men here.' Then she heard herself speak.

'Did you notice how many policemen there were?' she asked.

'I couldn't see them all,' he said. 'About half a dozen, I should think. Why d'you ask?'

'Well, you have three or four, I suppose. I hope there won't be a shoot-up.'

'If there's a shoot-up,' said Costello, 'it will start with you. If your husband knows what's good for him and good for you, he'll get rid of those half dozen policemen.'

As he went towards the front door Graham was also thinking hard, but in his case there was no time for wondering why he'd found himself in this present position, or for wondering how people in the same position might have dealt with it. He'd got to find some way of preserving Harriet's and his lives. He opened the door. Superintendent Ackroyd was there.

'Oh, Mr Ackroyd,' said Graham, 'or is it Superintendent now?'

'It is, as a matter of fact. How are you, Mr Simpkins? May I come in?'

'Yes, do.'

The superintendent came in and Graham shut the door.

'Do sit down, superintendent.'

The superintendent sat. 'Nice little place you've got here,' he said.

'It is rather.'

'Is your wife at home?'

'No, I'm afraid not. She's gone to see her sister.'

'Well, how are you? It's a long time since we met.'

'Very well indeed, thank you,' said Graham. 'It didn't do me any harm to lose quite a bit of weight during the last seven years.'

'Have you any idea why I've come to see you?' asked the superintendent.

'Well, Miss Clinch of the Citizens' Protection Association has been here already and from what she said your visit doesn't altogether surprise me.'

'Miss Clinch, eh? She doesn't waste much time. I've come for several reasons and I think I can fairly say that all of them are for your benefit. That's a very nice picture you have up there. Is it a Monet?'

'It's a copy, as a matter of fact. A friend of mine did it. You didn't think it was an original by any chance?'

'If you've kept a million and a half pounds you could afford it.'

'So that's what you've come about.'

'Partly. But first of all I want to get one thing plain. I'm not making any bargain with you now. You can tell your solicitor or Miss Clinch or whoever you like about this conversation, but I'm making it plain there will be no bargain between us.'

'Quite so, superintendent,' said Graham. 'No bargain of any kind.'

'There are three things I'm concerned with. First of all, I want every scrap of information you can give me about the identity or whereabouts of the people who actually took the money.'

'I thought it was me,' said Graham.

'We'll come to that in a moment. Secondly, I want to know what you did with the money and where it is now. And thirdly, as Miss Clinch has probably told you, we have evidence which we are prepared to put forward to the Home Secretary or the Court of Appeal or both that you were not yourself concerned in the raid and that your fingerprints were falsely placed on the safe in order to make it appear that you were.'

'It's all very nice and friendly of you, superintendent. What next?'

'A million and a half pounds is a lot of money. I have been authorised by the bank to say that, if you will give information which will result in the apprehension of one or more of the ringleaders and the recovery of at least five hundred thousand pounds, they will pay you fifty thousand pounds.'

'That's ten per cent,' said Graham. 'What you might call a service charge. Suppose I were able to give you information, I don't say that I can, but supposing I were able to give you information that would enable you to recover the full, or nearly the full, one and a half million pounds, will I get ten per cent on that?'

'They are prepared to pay a further five per cent on anything over half a million pounds.'

'That's a promise, is it?' said Graham. 'I thought you said there was to be no bargaining between us.'

'It isn't between us. It's a promise by the bank and you can take it that, if you give them the necessary information, it will be paid.'

'Suppose,' said Graham, 'just suppose, I could tell you where the money was but not who the ringleaders were or who they are. What would I get for that?'

'Nothing so far as I'm concerned,' said the superintendent. 'You could ask the bank what they would do, but I fancy their attitude would be that a promise which didn't provide for the arrest of one or more of the gang would come near to what used to be called compounding a felony. By the way, you may be interested to know that since you were convicted the difference between a felony and a misdemeanour has been abolished.'

'Yes, they told us in prison. I need hardly tell you that we talked of little else for the next fortnight.'

'Well now, what can you tell us? What were the names of the people concerned in the raid? We've a good idea we know the man who instigated the whole affair.'

'That's interesting,' said Graham. 'What was his name?'

'A man called Costello.'

'How d'you spell it?' asked Graham.

'C-o-s-t-e-l-l-o.'

'Never heard of him.'

'Are you sure of that?' asked the superintendent.

'Absolutely.'

'He's an educated rogue. Went to a public school and Cambridge University.'

'Did he distinguish himself there?'

'He got a half blue for billiards, as a matter of fact. He's a clever devil. He always gets other people to do the dirty work, so he's got no form. We've every reason to believe that he lives abroad in a country with which we've got no extradition treaty. But the reason I've come here today so soon after your release is that we thought he might be interested to pay you a call too. Are you sure you don't know him?'

'Absolutely certain.'

'I should warn you that he's a very dangerous man. Although he doesn't usually appear in the front line himself, he isn't frightened to use a gun. We believe that he got rid of one or two of his gang who may have got awkward or wanted more than their fair share.'

'What should I do if he does come?'

'Well, he may not come here himself in the first instance. He may get somebody else to spy out the land.

On the other hand, if he hasn't already got the million and a half, he wants it very badly and he won't want to share it with anyone. So he might come just by himself with a bodyguard.'

'That still doesn't tell me what I should do.'

'I'll tell you. That's why I'm here. I've got a couple of radio engineers outside. And they're going to fix you up with press buttons all over the house. As soon as he comes in – '

'I shan't recognise him,' put in Graham.

'Well, as soon as you recognise who he is – and if you're in any doubt assume he is the man – press one of these buttons and this will alert a police car which is just nearby. You keep him talking and we'll do the rest.'

'It's a little alarming,' said Graham.

'I'm afraid it is,' said the superintendent, 'but it's the best we can do.'

'But if you have the house watched, why can't you pick him up before he comes into it?'

'For the simple reason,' said the superintendent, 'that we haven't got any evidence against him. Now I've got a little tape recorder here which you can conceal in a drawer. It's extremely receptive and will pick up any voice in the room. I'll put it here now.'

The superintendent got up, opened a drawer and put an instrument inside it.

'There's a little button which I'll put under the desk. All you've got to do is to press that button and that will start the thing working. It can go on for an hour and a half. Just keep him talking and he's bound to give himself away. He's come for the money and he's bound to ask where it is.'

'But this man's dangerous,' said Graham, 'and is liable to shoot me.'

'I'm afraid that is so,' said the superintendent.

'I was a good deal safer in prison.'

'I'm not sure that you were,' said the superintendent. 'People like Costello have their agents all over the place. And that includes the inside of a prison. They may have approached you already.'

'Not to my knowledge,' said Graham. 'But I think I'd prefer you to arrest the man before he comes to the house.'

'There are no grounds for arresting him.'

'So what you're really doing is to use me as a decoy.'

'I'm not using you,' said the superintendent. 'You're a ready-made decoy, if you like. If he hasn't got that one and a half million pounds and he thinks you know where it is, he'll be after it like a shot. Forgive me for using that word. I'm surprised he hasn't been here already.'

'No,' said Graham, 'I've had a most peaceful and uneventful morning. But from what you say things are likely to move pretty fast from now on.'

'They are indeed. Now, let's get down to brass tacks.'

'I'd rather you didn't use that expression, superintendent.'

'Why on earth not?'

'It reminds me of a rather unpleasant interview I once had.'

'Never mind about that. Do you or do you not know where the money is?'

'If I did know, there wouldn't be much point in my telling you, unless I could also tell you the identity or whereabouts of one or more of the people you want to arrest. I've done my time. Why on earth should I help the bank if I don't get anything in return?'

'I can tell you that,' said the superintendent. 'In the first place you've got a duty to do so. In the second, I don't say they will but, if the bank got the money back, I think they'd want to do something to show their appreciation.'

'How much?'

'That's for them to say. I can't promise that they'd say anything.'

'Tell me something else, superintendent. D'you believe that I am completely innocent?'

'I can say this,' said the superintendent, 'I believe you were innocent of the charge you were convicted of but I also believe that you know where the money is.'

'Will I get compensation if my conviction is quashed?'

'Not if you've got the one and a half million pounds. After all, it's just as much stealing to hang on to the bank's money even if you didn't take it in the first instance. But if you hand it over and help us to get one of the ringleaders, you won't do too badly. A hundred thousand pounds wouldn't be too bad even at today's values. Now let's try the tape recorder and see if it's working.' The superintendent opened the drawer, pressed the button to start the tape recorder and then said: 'Let's check it to see if it works. You just say something.'

'What?' said Graham.

'Anything.'

'I'm so grateful for your coming here to see me, superintendent. Will that do?'

'Splendidly. Say something else.'

'I'm not in the least anxious or afraid.'

'Why d'you say that?'

'You asked me to say something and those were the words that just came into my head.'

'Right. That's enough. Let's try.' He opened the drawer, took out the tape recorder, pressed the switch to turn it back and then started it. The sound of the short conversation which they'd just had was clearly recorded. 'Well, that's all right, so you know what to do. Press it as soon as he comes in. If it's the wrong man, it doesn't matter. The important thing is to get a recording of everything that's said to you by any stranger who comes here.'

'Suppose he threatens to shoot me as soon as he comes in?'

'Well,' said the superintendent, 'provided you've pressed one of the many buttons which you'll have all over the house, a police car will arrive here within a very few minutes.'

'He may have shot me by then.'

'He won't shoot you while there's any chance of your giving him the information which he wants. There's no point in his just killing you. A chap like Costello doesn't kill for fun, so what you've got to do, if he threatens to shoot you, is to keep him in conversation as long as you possibly can. If you know where the money is, for example, start telling him where it is and how to get hold of it. Go along with him the whole time. Appear anxious to do everything that he wants you to do. That way you ought to be able to keep him going for ten minutes. And that will be quite enough to have the place surrounded.'

'That's all very well,' said Graham, 'but, if he knows the place is surrounded, he'll use me as a hostage and threaten to kill me unless you provide him with the money and a getaway car and all the rest of it. What do I do then?'

'First of all,' said the superintendent, 'leave the door on the latch so that our people can burst into the room at a moment's notice.'

'Then there may be a shooting match.'

'That's perfectly true, but you're less likely to be killed in a shooting match than you will be if you're a hostage.'

'I must confess I don't like it at all,' said Graham. 'I'd much prefer you to arrest the man before he can get at me.'

'I've told you we can't,' said the superintendent. 'We've no evidence against him.'

'Does the Home Secretary know you're here now?'

'I've no idea. I don't take him into my confidence. I get my orders from my superior officer and I'm carrying them out. Whether he's communicated with the Home Secretary I've absolutely no idea. It's none of my business.'

'When d'you think he's likely to come?' said Graham.

'Your guess is as good as mine,' said the superintendent, 'but if my information is correct it'll be pretty soon. At any rate we're going to keep a twenty-four hour watch from now on. Tell me,' he added, 'is there any other way out of the house except through the front door?'

'Only the windows,' said Graham, 'and the ones at the back are too small for a man to get through. You can get through the front windows in the sitting room – over there,' and he pointed towards the door which was ajar.

'That's good,' said the superintendent. 'Leave this front door here closed but on the latch.'

'All night?' asked Graham. 'I don't quite like the idea of that.'

'I could leave a man behind here if that would make you feel any happier.'

'It would a great deal,' said Graham. 'He'd be armed, I suppose?'

'Oh yes.'

'Why can't you do that in any event? Why not leave a couple of your men? In the next room. I'd certainly feel much happier if you did.'

'I don't see why not,' said the superintendent.

As the superintendent said this, Harriet, listening next door with Costello, saw him motion her to come nearer to him. He turned her round and pointed the barrel of the revolver into her back so that she wished she could have fainted.

CHAPTER TEN

Use for a Monet

'I'm glad you like that picture, superintendent,' said Graham, pointing to the copy of the Monet. 'Personally I think it's a very clever copy. From my point of view, if it's a good copy, that's almost as good as having the real thing. The original cost a hundred thousand pounds possibly. If I'd paid for this copy, I suppose it would have cost me about fifteen. As it is, I got it for nothing. I think he's put on the paint extraordinarily well. Have a closer look if you'd like.'

'Thanks,' said the superintendent, 'I will. I do a little painting myself.'

'How interesting,' said Graham. 'Tell me frankly. D'you think you could have done it as well yourself?'

The superintendent got up and started to examine the Monet. After he'd been looking at it for a few seconds he heard Graham open and shut a drawer. He thought nothing of this until a moment later he felt what might well have been the barrel of a revolver in his back and then he heard Graham say: 'Put your hands up, superintendent. At once, please. I mean this. This is loaded and there's a silencer on it.'

'What the hell d'you think you're doing?' said the superintendent.

'Never mind about that,' said Graham. 'Put your hands up at once.' He emphasised the 'at once' with as much menace as he could get into his voice. The superintendent complied. As soon as his hands were up, Graham felt the outside of the superintendent's pockets and then, with the speed of a pickpocket, he took out the superintendent's gun from one of them and put it in one of his own pockets.

'I'm sorry about this,' said Graham, 'but you left me no alternative.' Then he called out to Costello. 'It's all right,' he shouted, 'you can come out now. He's not armed.'

Costello and Harriet came slowly into the room, Costello holding his gun. Graham put down the pencil which he had held into the superintendent's back.

'First of all,' said Graham, 'I think we might disconnect this little thing.' He took out the tape recorder from the drawer, pulled away the button and Sellotape from below the drawer. 'A nice little gadget, don't you think? Now, superintendent,' he went on, 'how many men have you got outside?'

'Three.'

'Are they armed?'

'Yes.'

'Well, if you want to live through this little affair, superintendent, you've got to do exactly what you're told. Any false move and you're a dead man. Is that understood?'

'I hear what you say,' said the superintendent.

'Now, I'm not going to take any chances,' said Graham. 'Are all your men in the car?'

'Yes.'

Graham turned to Costello. 'What I suggest is that we let him open the door, keeping him fully covered, and, when we've done that, he is to tell his men to go away and to report to him later at, say, Scotland Yard. Now, superintendent, if they don't go away or if you say anything else to them or give any sort of warning you'll be shot.'

Graham looked at Costello. 'How will that do?'

'Not bad,' said Costello. 'I must say you're learning.'

'I've had a good lesson,' said Graham. 'Right, superintendent, are you ready? Now we'll stand back here,' and he indicated the entrance to the sitting room. 'When I say the word "Move", open the door wide, shout to your driver to go away and to report to you later at Scotland Yard. Are you going to do that?'

'I don't seem to have any choice,' said the superintendent.

'You haven't,' said Graham. 'No choice whatever. Don't do a thing until I say "Move" and, when I do, just open the door and stay just inside it. If you attempt to go out of it, you'll be shot. Now are you ready?'

'Yes,' said the superintendent.

'Right,' said Graham. He paused for a few seconds, then he said: 'Move.' As the superintendent did not move immediately, he repeated the command. The superintendent threw open the door and called: 'Grant.'

The driver jumped out of the car and answered: 'Yes, sir?'

'You can all go off now,' said the superintendent. 'I shall be here some time. Report to me later at Scotland Yard. Is that plain?'

'When, sir?' asked the driver.

'Say at half past four this afternoon. All right?'

'Yes, sir.'

'That'll do,' said Graham very quietly. 'Now shut the door.'

The superintendent obeyed and a few moments later the car could be heard starting up and driving away.

'Not bad for a beginner,' said Graham.

'Not at all bad,' said Costello.

'I think we'd better tie him up now,' said Graham. 'Don't you agree? Did you leave the cord in the other room? I'll get it.'

Graham went to the other room and came back with the cord.

'You can use this much better than I can,' he said, and threw the cord over to Costello. In order to catch it Costello lowered his gun. Graham immediately took out the superintendent's gun from his pocket and handed it to him.

'This is yours, I believe,' he said.

'Drop that,' said the superintendent to Costello, 'or I'll shoot. Come on. At once.'

Costello saw that there was no alternative and dropped his gun. Graham went and picked it up.

'He's got several men outside,' he said.

'Keep your hands up and stand over against that wall,' said the superintendent. Still aiming at him, the superintendent went to the telephone and dialled 999.

'When you've done that,' said Graham, 'you're going to want the Midland Bank at Liverpool to hold the man who produces my authority to collect the package which contains the keys to the three safe deposits.'

'Right,' said the superintendent.

At that moment the telephonist answered.

'This is Superintendent Ackroyd of the CID, speaking. Send all available cars to The Cottage, London Lane, Redgrave at once. There are some men outside who are probably armed. There's one inside but I can take care of him. Is that clear? Please repeat it.' The telephonist repeated it. 'Right.'

The superintendent replaced the receiver.

'While I cover him, would you kindly put these handcuffs on him,' he said to Graham, as he produced a pair from one of his pockets. 'Costello, put your hands behind your back.'

Costello did as he was told and half a minute later he was duly handcuffed.

'That was pretty good work, Simpkins,' said the superintendent.

'What about the fellows outside?' asked Graham.

'I suspect that they'll either run away when they see the police cars arrive or my men will pick them up. I doubt if they'll shoot it out. Think they will, Costello?'

'I don't suppose so,' said Costello.

'D'you think we could relax now?' said Graham.

'Well, you can anyway,' said the superintendent.

'Thank you,' said Graham, and proceeded to slip on to the floor in a faint. Harriet went on her knees beside him.

'He'll be all right,' said the superintendent. 'It's a hysterical faint. Just put his head between his knees and he'll soon come to. I'm not surprised in view of all that's happened to him.'

Harriet began to speak soothingly to Graham. 'Are you all right, darling?' she said.

He started to regain consciousness and mumbled something which no one could hear.

'What did you say, darling?' said Harriet.

'I'm terribly sorry,' said Graham very faintly, 'but I forgot the digestive biscuits.'

Henry Cecil

According to the Evidence

Alec Morland is on trial for murder. He has tried to remedy the ineffectiveness of the law by taking matters into his own hands. Unfortunately for him, his alleged crime was not committed in immediate defence of others or of himself. In this fascinating murder trial you will not find out until the very end just how the law will interpret his actions. Will his defence be accepted or does a different fate await him?

The Asking Price

Ronald Holbrook is a fifty-seven-year-old bachelor who has lived in the same house for twenty years. Jane Doughty, the daughter of his next-door neighbours, is seventeen. She suddenly decides she is in love with Ronald and wants to marry him. Everyone is amused at first but then events take a disturbingly sinister turn and Ronald finds himself enmeshed in a potentially tragic situation.

'The secret of Mr Cecil's success lies in continuing to do superbly what everyone now knows he can do well.'
The Sunday Times

Henry Cecil

Brief Tales from the Bench

What does it feel like to be a Judge? Read these stories and you can almost feel you are looking at proceedings from the lofty position of the Bench.

With a collection of eccentric and amusing characters, Henry Cecil brings to life the trials in a County Court and exposes the complex and often contradictory workings of the English legal system.

'Immensely readable. His stories rely above all on one quality – an extraordinary, an arresting, a really staggering ingenuity.'
New Statesman

Brothers in Law

Roger Thursby, aged twenty-four, is called to the bar. He is young, inexperienced and his love life is complicated. He blunders his way through a succession of comic adventures including his calamitous debut at the bar.

His career takes an upward turn when he is chosen to defend the caddish Alfred Green at the Old Bailey. In this first Roger Thursby novel Henry Cecil satirizes the legal profession with his usual wit and insight.

'Uproariously funny.' *The Times*

'Full of charm and humour. I think it is the best Henry Cecil yet.' P G Wodehouse

HENRY CECIL

SOBER AS A JUDGE

Roger Thursby, the hero of *Brothers in Law* and *Friends at Court*, continues his career as a High Court judge. He presides over a series of unusual cases, including a professional debtor and an action about a consignment of oranges which turned to juice before delivery. There is a delightful succession of eccentric witnesses as the reader views proceedings from the Bench.

'The author's gift for brilliant characterisation makes this a book that will delight lawyers and laymen as much as did its predecessors.' *The Daily Telegraph*

THE WANTED MAN

When Norman Partridge moves to Little Bacon, a pretty country village, he proves to be a kind and helpful neighbour and is liked by everyone. Initially it didn't seem to matter that no one knew anything about his past or how he managed to live so comfortably without having to work.

Six months before, John Gladstone, a wealthy bank-robber had escaped from custody. Gradually, however, Partridge's neighbours begin to ask themselves questions. Was it mere coincidence that Norman Partridge had the build and features of the escaped convict? While some villagers are suspicious but reluctant to report their concerns to the police, others decide to take matters into their own hands…

OTHER TITLES BY HENRY CECIL AVAILABLE DIRECT
FROM HOUSE OF STRATUS

Quantity		£	$(US)	$(CAN)	€
	ACCORDING TO THE EVIDENCE	6.99	11.50	15.99	11.50
	ALIBI FOR A JUDGE	6.99	11.50	15.99	11.50
	THE ASKING PRICE	6.99	11.50	15.99	11.50
	BRIEF TALES FROM THE BENCH	6.99	11.50	15.99	11.50
	BROTHERS IN LAW	6.99	11.50	15.99	11.50
	THE BUTTERCUP SPELL	6.99	11.50	15.99	11.50
	CROSS PURPOSES	6.99	11.50	15.99	11.50
	DAUGHTERS IN LAW	6.99	11.50	15.99	11.50
	FATHERS IN LAW	6.99	11.50	15.99	11.50
	FRIENDS AT COURT	6.99	11.50	15.99	11.50
	FULL CIRCLE	6.99	11.50	15.99	11.50
	INDEPENDENT WITNESS	6.99	11.50	15.99	11.50
	MUCH IN EVIDENCE	6.99	11.50	15.99	11.50

ALL HOUSE OF STRATUS BOOKS ARE AVAILABLE FROM GOOD BOOKSHOPS OR
DIRECT FROM THE PUBLISHER:

Internet: **www.houseofstratus.com** including author interviews, reviews, features.

Email: **sales@houseofstratus.com** please quote author, title and credit card details.

OTHER TITLES BY HENRY CECIL AVAILABLE DIRECT
FROM HOUSE OF STRATUS

Quantity		£	$(US)	$(CAN)	€
	Natural Causes	6.99	11.50	15.99	11.50
	No Bail for the Judge	6.99	11.50	15.99	11.50
	No Fear or Favour	6.99	11.50	15.99	11.50
	The Painswick Line	6.99	11.50	15.99	11.50
	Portrait of a Judge	6.99	11.50	15.99	11.50
	Settled Out of Court	6.99	11.50	15.99	11.50
	Sober as a Judge	6.99	11.50	15.99	11.50
	Tell you What I'll do	6.99	11.50	15.99	11.50
	Truth With Her Boots On	6.99	11.50	15.99	11.50
	Unlawful Occasions	6.99	11.50	15.99	11.50
	The Wanted Man	6.99	11.50	15.99	11.50
	Ways and Means	6.99	11.50	15.99	11.50
	A Woman Named Anne	6.99	11.50	15.99	11.50

ALL HOUSE OF STRATUS BOOKS ARE AVAILABLE FROM GOOD BOOKSHOPS OR
DIRECT FROM THE PUBLISHER:

Hotline: UK ONLY: **0800 169 1780**, please quote author, title and credit card
details.
INTERNATIONAL: **+44 (0) 20 7494 6400**, please quote author, title,
and credit card details.

Send to: **House of Stratus**
24c Old Burlington Street
London
W1X 1RL
UK

Please allow following carriage costs per ORDER
(For goods up to free carriage limits shown)

	£(Sterling)	$(US)	$(CAN)	€(Euros)
UK	1.95	3.20	4.29	3.00
Europe	2.95	4.99	6.49	5.00
North America	2.95	4.99	6.49	5.00
Rest of World	2.95	5.99	7.75	6.00
Free carriage for goods value over:	50	75	100	75

PLEASE SEND CHEQUE, POSTAL ORDER (STERLING ONLY), EUROCHEQUE, OR
INTERNATIONAL MONEY ORDER (PLEASE CIRCLE METHOD OF PAYMENT YOU WISH TO USE)
MAKE PAYABLE TO: STRATUS HOLDINGS plc

Order total including postage:_____Please tick currency you wish to use and add total amount of order:

☐ £ (Sterling)   ☐ $ (US)   ☐ $ (CAN)   ☐ € (EUROS)

VISA, MASTERCARD, SWITCH, AMEX, SOLO, JCB:

☐☐☐☐☐☐☐☐☐☐☐☐☐☐☐☐☐☐☐☐☐☐☐☐☐

Issue number (Switch only):

☐☐☐

Start Date: **Expiry Date:**

☐☐/☐☐   ☐☐/☐☐

Signature: _____

NAME: _____

ADDRESS: _____

_____

POSTCODE: _____

Please allow 28 days for delivery.

Prices subject to change without notice.
Please tick box if you do not wish to receive any additional information. ☐

House of Stratus publishes many other titles in this genre; please check our website (**www.houseofstratus.com**) for more details